Tuesday's Grace

A Modern Day Miracle

Sara M. Howard

Edited by Crystal Bowman

xulon
PRESS

Tuesday's Grace
A Modern Day Miracle
by Sara M. Howard

Printed in the United States of America

ISBN 9781612155890

The names of places, professionals, and birth family have been changed for privacy purposes.

Front cover photo taken by Sara M. Howard. Pictured are Evan and Grace.

Edited by Crystal Bowman

Final copyediting by Jeff Harryman

Photo formatting by Brian Fidler

www.xulonpress.com

Dedication

To my amazing Grace: May you never forget all of the details of your story and the touch of God on your life.

"Only be careful, and watch yourselves closely so that you do not forget the things your eyes have seen or let them slip from your heart as long as you live. Teach them to your children and to their children after them" (Deuteronomy 4:9).

Table of Contents

Introduction

The Purpose

Due to the recent events in my life, a few people have asked me to write a story about what has happened. Many have asked about the details of our story. I have wanted to tell everyone every detail of this story because each part is so incredible. But there are many things to tell. I cannot remember all of it without looking back at my writings. Thankfully, I kept a journal recording details during two unbelievable months. Writing helped me cope during difficult times. But I am also glad that I recorded all of the developments as they occurred, or I may not have believed my own story.

I will warn you now—this story is very emotional. I am not always this emotional, but there were many events in a short period of time that evoked sorrow, joy, and amazement. These events deserve strong emotions. I know there are many true and astonishing stories that occur every day. I know many people have stories that would make us gasp from sadness or amazement. Some people claim to see angels or audibly hear the voice of God. Many have lost children or family members too soon. Many have been through chronic illness and have experienced a miracle. There are those whose lives are continual stories of great success, fame, or fortune. There are books about those who have had a near-death experience; I love those stories. Because of all the stories out there, I wondered if anyone would want to read this story. No one in this story visually sees heaven or becomes rich and famous. But I know this story is special. Sharing this story has affected the lives of other people. I decided to share it with as many people as I can. It is a true story and it is an incredible story. I want people to find hope in knowing that miracles still happen today. I personally never want to forget the details of this story. I have also discovered I love to write. So, here we are. Now you know my purpose for writing this book. You are getting ready to read about real people who live real lives. This is about real events that led up to a modern day miracle.

Sara M. Howard

CHAPTER ONE

A Heart Stopper

The large operating room was filled with busy people. At least ten sets of blue surgical booties swished across the floor. The air was cold, lights were bright, and sounds were minimal. Specialists were there: three doctors to operate on Lizzy, many nurses, and several surgical techs. A neonatologist and his team were there to receive the expected baby. Everyone was quietly moving around the room, each doing a different job. I had never seen so many people in one operating room before, and being a nurse, I have been in several. The nurses placed the blue drape across Lizzy's chest. I was standing by Lizzy, offering support and holding her hand. Her blonde hair was pulled off of her cream-colored skin by her blue surgical bonnet. She kept looking at me with fearful glances while she grimaced and squeezed my sweaty hand tightly enough to turn my fingers white. I did not mind. I had a special place in my heart for Lizzy. I kept looking across the bed at my strong husband while he stood near, taking everything in. My husband and I did not speak words, but our eyes enabled us to communicate. The anesthesiologist and the surgeons explained often what they were doing. The team for the baby was standing in the corner with equipment ready and waiting. I knew we were getting the best care we could. It was all going just as planned. I stood up and peeked over the drape. I saw the baby's head. I took a long deep breath. I waited for just a small cry to break the silence of the room. I think my heart stopped beating then.

In moments that seemed to last an eternity, many thoughts rushed through my mind: *I cannot believe we are here in this operating room. How did this happen so fast? What is going to happen next? Are we getting ready to witness a life or a death?*

CHAPTER 2

A Little History

My husband Josh and I grew up in the same small suburb just a thirty-minute drive from a large city. We went to the same school and had the same friends. We both had a happy childhood and were raised in strong, supportive families. Josh and I "liked each other" in the fifth grade and then again in the eighth grade. Then we started dating our junior year in high school and wanted to be together all the time. We stayed together through our college years despite attending different colleges for a time. We had so many life plans—go to college, get married, make money, buy a house, and have a family—the perfect life. It was the Midwest dream and all was well.

In my fourth and last year of nursing school, we had the perfect wedding on the beach in the Bahamas. My high school sweetheart was also the man of my dreams. Being around other boys in college reinforced that Josh was the only man for me. Josh was a great athlete and popular. He was 6'2" with blonde hair, big muscles, and gray-blue eyes. His looks were just a bonus. Josh had a calm demeanor with a big heart and always worked hard. Not much rattled him except talking about *Star Wars*. The most exciting part was that Josh loved me back.

After being married for a year, we bought our first home. It was the perfect older home to start a family. It was small, but still had three bedrooms—enough space for two children to have their own rooms. I had a great job as a dialysis nurse on an evening shift. Josh was working his way through pharmacy school with only a few years left. Everything was close to perfect, just as planned. After doing a lot of traveling—as many couples dream of doing—we were ready. It was time. Everything was in place. We were ready for a family.

As women we start to prepare for this moment from the time we are little girls. We play house and pretend we are mommies. We put baby dolls under our shirts to look pregnant, even though we are too young to know how babies are made. Then we start searching for the best man to become a daddy to our children.

For me, being a mom was something I always wanted to be. I think it is pre-wired in most women, and we start preparing at a very young age. Both Josh and I always knew we wanted a family. It was never a question. It was in our plan.

CHAPTER THREE

Feeling Some Heartache

As time went by, many of our friends and family members were starting their families. But it just wasn't happening for us. Our home was organized, clean, and quiet—too quiet. We felt an emptiness and loneliness. I had a deep ache in my heart that only someone who has yearned for a child could understand. Josh also had a lot of pain and trouble accepting that infertility was our reality.

With each infertility treatment our specialist believed pregnancy would happen for us; everything appeared to be just right for conception. There were many tests, drugs, and a surgery. Our specialist said there was no explanation for the infertility. He believed pregnancy would happen with time. But pregnancy never did happen, even with modern treatments and the confident opinion of a specialist.

At this stage in our lives, everything seemed to be about babies—baby showers, diaper commercials, and pregnant women everywhere. I prayed that when I told my pregnant friends congratulations they could not see the tears forming in my eyes. I really was happy for them, but I longed to be them at that moment. They were feeling life inside of them. They got to experience birth—the most amazing life experience most women say they have had—an experience I longed to have but knew I never would.

I felt angry when I heard women complain about being pregnant or taking care of their children. When learning about my infertility, some women actually said, "You can have my children." Fire burned inside me when I heard those comments, and I wanted to hit the women right in the face and ask them if they realized who they were talking to. I pictured my fist landing right between the eyes hard enough to knock the women off their feet. I loved to picture the shocked looks on their faces. I often thought about offering to take their children if they would sign the papers. I knew those women did not realize how much their words stung.

I knew that pregnancy and raising children was not all fun and gumdrops. We were close with our nieces and nephews, so we had seen the real child-rearing show. I knew all about sleepless nights, temper tantrums, poopy pants, and baby spit-up. I just wanted these women to realize the precious gift they had been given. My empty arms ached.

I questioned God about the things that didn't make sense to me. *Why were there so many unplanned babies born to young girls who were unprepared to be mothers? Why did some mothers see their kids as a burden rather than a blessing?* It hurt me to hear mothers screaming at their kids in public, and I wondered what happened to those children at home? It just did not seem to make sense.

Josh and I spent a lot of time asking God to take away the pain and emptiness. We could not imagine having no children in our home. I spent a lot of time on my knees sobbing and asking God to help me accept that I was not in control. I asked Him to help me accept that just because I made a plan didn't mean it was going to happen. I still remember the moment and the place where I changed my prayer from begging God for a child to asking Him to help us accept His plan for our lives. I felt a burden lifted. I was relieved that we no longer had to endure the rollercoaster ride that each month brought. We would start with great hopes and end in a downhill ride of sadness, then back up, back down. That was all over. I felt new hope. But we could not have imagined the amazing things that God had planned for us.

CHAPTER FOUR

The Journey of Adoption

We pursued adoption as a way to start our family. A number of months later my sister, Stephanie, brought us a pamphlet about an adoption meeting from a church that her family had just visited. We went to that meeting, and the divine work of God started kicking in. The right people were in the right places at the right time. We were referred to an agency by a couple at the meeting. We contacted that agency and started with the basics that everyone who adopts needs to go through. Soon, our social worker knew us better than we knew ourselves. We knew if we had any skeletons in the closet that we had forgotten about, our social worker would find them!

The agency requested reference letters and letters from employers. The agency also requested birth certificates, a marriage license, fingerprints, background checks, physical assessments, etc. There were times when we felt more like criminals than prospective parents! Everyone looked at us under the microscope—the agencies, the social workers, the lawyers, the judge, and the birth family. We knew we had flaws just like everyone has flaws. We wondered if those flaws would matter.

Another big concern and stressor was the financial aspect of adoption. It is very difficult to find loans to pay for thousands of dollars in adoption fees. We knew that our child would be worth every penny we would have to pay, but the reality was that we'd have to figure out a way to pay. We could not find the loans we needed, so we took a second mortgage on our house and used multiple credit cards. There were some tax breaks to help offset adoption costs, but we had to wait until tax return time to receive that help.

We had to jump through many hoops and hire numerous lawyers to prove we could be good parents. With all of the interrogation, we began to wonder and question ourselves. *Will we be good parents? Maybe God did not want us to be parents.* The doubts kept creeping in.

One year and one month after all of the daunting questions and stressful process, we had a new son! At three months old, little Evan came to live in our quiet, organized, and waiting home. We were the happiest people on earth! We cried and cried, but they were tears of joy. We were so thankful to have a baby boy to love and hold. Our home was no longer lonely. God had answered our prayers, but it wasn't an easy journey.

There were more questions and complications beyond the normal process with Evan's adoption journey. It took us over a month to get him moved from his foster home into our home because of incorrect paperwork and legal hang-ups. Thankfully, he had wonderful foster parents! We traveled to visit him at his foster home during this difficult waiting period. It was stressful enough that I lost twenty pounds in a month's time. This soon came to be known among my friends and family as the adoption diet. It's not a healthy way to lose weight—so I told my friends not to try the adoption diet plan!

Eventually, things worked out well, and it was obvious that God's hand was in it and that Evan was meant to be with us forever. He is our gift from God—adorable, loving, and spirited—the little boy we had wanted for so long.

We had prayed for a family and the ups and downs that come along with it. God began forming our family through the gift of adoption. Through this adoption journey with all of its trials, Josh and I grew closer. Our extended family was by our side. All of our relationships grew stronger. God had a much better plan than we did. Our view of God's plan versus our plan completely changed. What we didn't realize at the time was that everything we endured to adopt Evan was just a stepping stone to prepare us for our next adoption and the challenges it would bring.

CHAPTER FIVE

A Second Child?

Josh and I both knew that we wanted a second child. We had talked about possibly starting the adoption process when Evan was around age two or three. But when Evan was almost four, we still had not started the process again. I guess there were things that we wanted to have in place—a little more room in the house, a little more money saved, a little more time to spend with Evan. We wanted to adopt again but kept putting it off. I realized that if we waited until everything was perfect we'd be eighty years old by the time we were ready! I wanted to have another child, but I dreaded and feared going through the adoption process and all of the paperwork again. I kept thinking, *What if the social worker or judge thinks we're not doing a good job with Evan?* Parenting is hard enough without having everything you do as parents be evaluated and judged by others. I dreaded having to go under oath and being put on the stand—literally. *What if they think we are not good enough? What if our finances look bad to them?* There were so many fears. Maybe one child was all God had planned for our family.

I was wrong. In September of 2007, I went to Dallas for a class to learn more about peritoneal dialysis for my job. I had been a dialysis nurse for over eight years, and I did some occasional traveling. I was in a car with three other medical professionals. Sally was newer to our company, and I did not know her very well. Sally talked about her family, and I talked about mine. I showed her pictures of our handsome little Evan, as I was really missing him. We looked at his dark brown hair, hazel eyes, and freckled nose. I love the "shreckles" as Evan would call them.

As we discussed Evan's adoption, Sally told me several details about a pregnant young woman, Carly, who was in difficult circumstances and considering adoption as an option for her unborn baby. This young woman was a close friend of Sally. I tried not to act too excited, even though I wanted to bust out of my seat belt! I had a feeling this was not just coincidence. I just listened, trying not to ask too many questions.

That night I called Josh to tell him about this young woman. We called Sally a few days later to let her know we were both interested in a second adoption. A month later, at another work meeting, Sally informed me that Carly was really leaning toward adoption and asked if she could tell this young woman about our family. The answer was a big *yes*! The baby was due in January, which was only one month away. It seemed so sudden. We didn't know if we could have all of the paperwork and criminal background checks completed by that time. We called the agency that we used with Evan and discussed what we should do. They recommended that we go ahead and get everything completed so we would not miss this opportunity. Our social worker, Mallory, informed us that it would be much less costly and much less paperwork than our first home study because some of our old records were still good. It was a hard decision to move forward because Carly was wavering in her decision. We knew it would cost money to move forward, and there were no guarantees. We had to take a leap of faith with a lot of prayer.

It was Christmastime, and the house was full of Christmas decorations and lights. It was the season of joy and hope. We talked with Sally often, getting updates on Carly. We found out that she wanted to meet us. We rushed to get our fingerprints taken and medical exam forms completed. We gathered a few of the other various forms that we needed and scheduled our home study appointment.

We only had one week to prepare for our visit with Carly. After discussing it with Sally, we decided we would meet in our home. We talked over the details, wanting to be as prepared as possible. But I wondered how to prepare for a meeting like this. *Should I have snacks? Should the house look perfect or just a little lived in? Should we dress up or be casual? Should we ask a few questions, many, or none? Should Evan be there or not?* This meeting could change the future of our family and a little precious life. Throughout the day, I became more and more nervous. I was so nervous that I was sick to my stomach. Josh had it together and was pretty calm as usual.

The house was clean. The Christmas lights were glistening. Christmas music filled the rooms, and they smelled of cookies and cinnamon. My mom and dad were picking up Evan. We were ready. But a few hours before Sally and Carly were supposed to arrive, we received a text message that Carly had changed her mind about the adoption. We were stunned, even though we had wondered many times if Carly would change her mind. But, since we were so close to meeting her, we thought the meeting, at least, was a sure thing. We sat quietly in the living room and just looked at each other for a while. We talked about how sad we were and how we felt this was all just wasted time and energy.

After processing our emotions, Evan, Josh, and I took all of the carefully prepared snacks and had a party in our bedroom while we laughed at the movie *Elf.* We ate crackers, sausage, cheese, and fancy boxed Christmas cookies. Yum! Then we spent some time in prayer and felt much better. Prayer, laughter, and good food can do so much for the soul! It was just what we needed. We didn't know why or how, but we knew that God had some kind of plan with all of this.

Once again we were preparing our home for another to judge. On December 6, 2007, we had our home study scheduled with the social worker from our adoption agency. We thought about canceling the appointment; but all of our paperwork was finished, so we went ahead. Mallory was right. The process second time was so much easier. Now we were thinking a lot more about babies and wanting to add to our family.

The weather was calling for a snowstorm that day. I was afraid Mallory would have to cancel. I knew if we had to reschedule, it would be after the holidays until Josh and I could get another weekday off together. And sure enough—she made it! I did not feel as nervous about this visit since Mallory was the same social worker who did our home study with Evan, and we were looking forward to seeing her. She interviewed us and studied our home to see if we were prepared for another child.

We were a little worried about how Evan would respond to questions during the visit. At age three he liked to make up stories, and they were often embarrassing. We were not sure if he would answer questions at all, but he did. He loved talking to Mallory, and he even used good manners. We thought we had passed the embarrassing part until he shot himself with the Nerf gun and said, "Ouch! I shot my penis." Thank goodness Mallory thought it was hysterical!

The visit was actually relaxing. We sat on the living room floor drinking our coffee in front of the fireplace while we watched gigantic snowflakes fall over the grass and trees. We talked about our hopes of becoming parents again. Mallory spoke with a calm and quiet voice. She had a calming effect on us. She was also good at bringing out our emotions and getting us to share our feelings. She had had many years of practice and showed it. As we answered questions and talked about our future, we watched the snowflakes falling outside our living room windows. The grass changed from an ugly brown to a glistening white.

The snow began to blanket everything. We had a few other appointments that day, but they were canceled due to the weather. All we had to do before our paperwork was completed was to write a letter to the birthparents and create our adoption book. When we did Evan's book, it took us weeks. We had to copy and scan pictures. We had to get family members together to get pictures of everyone. We actually bought expensive software to get it to fit together nicely. This is something that adoptive parents really want to do well because it is often one of the first things that birthparents look at to help them choose a family for their baby. It's like a summary of your life and what it looks like.

Josh and I decided that snowy day was the perfect day to work on our letter and our adoption book. We had the time. The holidays and busy schedules were approaching fast. I had learned how to make an album online with digital photos. It was easy compared to what we had done before. We already had current pictures of our extended family in digital form. Josh and I agreed on everything we wrote and every picture we put in the book. We worked on it all day, and, to our own amazement, we finished. The day ended with Josh, Evan, and Kenzy, my niece, throwing snowballs and making a snowman in our front yard.

I wrote in my journal on December 12, 2007: *I told Josh how I believe that God has something in store for us soon. Everything today went so fast, smooth, and easy! It was as if God led us right to this perfect day. I cannot wait to meet this new baby that God knows is meant to be with us. I do believe that God has led us in this direction. And, if He thinks we can do it now, we can. If we are in His plan, then He will give us the strength and resources that we need.*

When I read that now, I get chills.

CHAPTER SIX

Two Paths Crossed

We celebrated the holidays with friends and family. We talked about what the New Year could bring for Josh, Evan, and me. My mom and dad, Mary and Steve, both lived in town. To Evan they are known as Maw Maw and Paw Paw. Josh's mom and dad, Jann and Bob, lived near us as well. They are known as Minny and Pa Pa Bob. My sister Stephanie, her husband Brian, and their kids, Andrew and Kenzy, lived only ten minutes away. And Josh's sister Rachel, her husband Chris, and their kids, Payton and Ava, lived about twenty minutes away. The kids' great-grandparents, Grandma Johnson, Grandma Daisy, Grandma Gorcie and Paw Paw John, Grandpa Don and Mary Alice, lived farther away, but we still saw most of them around the holidays. Having grandparents and great-grandparents made the holidays magical. We loved watching all of the kids go wild while they were showered with gifts. That Christmas was especially wonderful since we talked about the possibility of adding to our family. We answered questions about adoption and explained how we were waiting and expecting to hear something in a year or two. Everyone was very excited!

On Thursday January 24, 2008, it was sunny, but a cold negative three degrees Fahrenheit. It was a typical day around our house. Kenzy, our talkative five-year-old niece, had spent the night. It was a common thing for Kenzy to be with us or for Evan to be at my sister's house. All of the cousins are good friends.

The kids and I had been to the dentist, a fast-food place, and the library. We came home, and the kids started to watch a movie while I did some work in the office. My cell phone lay near me on the desk. It rang and displayed an odd number. I thought it might be Mallory since it was her area code. In that moment of thinking many things, I assumed she probably needed some more information to complete our home study paperwork. It really is amazing what can go through your mind before your phone rings three times. I answered the phone. The voice on the other side said, "I have some news for you."

I took a deep breath as my jaw dropped. Mallory went on to explain that a woman expecting a baby in May wanted to meet us. She began to tell us a little bit about her. She called her a beautiful angel. "The baby is a girl," she said. She explained that Lizzy had some very difficult circumstances in her life and knew that adoption was best for her baby. Lizzy had chosen a couple that were friends of a friend to adopt her baby. She had been going to Mallory for adoption counseling for months. When she met the couple that she had planned on choosing to adopt her baby, Lizzy became very uncomfortable with her decision.

Mallory encouraged Lizzy to come to her office and look at other couples she had on file. Lizzy told us later that our book was at the very bottom of the stack. She had asked to look at couples with no children first. Mallory said that Lizzy flew through all of them as if she were not really looking. Then she finally came to ours and started reading it. She asked for our full report and read that too. We were the only couple that Lizzy chose to meet. Mallory told us she knew we would be compatible.

I was in shock. The average wait with this agency is one-and-a half to two years. Our home study was not yet in its final draft. I was amazed our book was even completed in time for Lizzy to look at it. With Evan, we had waited a year for the call. Back then, every time a different area code would show up on our caller ID, we wondered if that could be the big call we were waiting for. We longed to hear the words, "I have some good news for you." Still stunned, I could not wait to tell Josh.

Josh was at work, and I could barely get my fingers to dial the right number. When he answered, I told him to go somewhere private. He went to his car and called back hours later. (Okay, it was really only minutes, but it felt like hours!) I told him the whole story, and he was in shock too. I started to call everyone in the family. No one answered—not one person! I had to leave messages. I could not believe it. My lifelong friend, Phoebe, was the first to know because she answered her phone. Slowly, the family started calling back, and I got to share the good news over and over.

I decided this was real enough to tell the kids. I told Evan and Kenzy. Evan's response was, "Cool." Later that day he said, "Yay, Mommy! We get a baby for me, for you, and for Daddy." He was glad it was a sister. Just the week before, he had told me that he prayed and asked God for a sister. This was not typical conversation for my little boy. It was another one of those moments that gives you chills. This was the first time Evan had ever told me that he had prayed to get something specific. God hears the prayers of three-year-olds.

Josh and I began talking a lot about meeting Lizzy. We were so excited that weekend that I could hardly eat because my stomach burned from excitement. We talked about what questions to ask. We reminded each other that we should not be nervous, but just be ourselves. I often tried telling myself not to get too excited so that I would not be disappointed. The nerves built up again as we got closer and closer to our meeting with Lizzy. Then the doubts crept in. *Will the meeting really happen, or will it get canceled at the last minute again?*

The meeting day soon arrived. We were supposed to meet at Mallory's office. This was a little easier than having someone come to the house. After we were all dressed, in the clothing that was well thought out, the phone rang. It was Mallory's phone number. *Here we go again,* I thought to myself. I figured that Lizzy had canceled or changed her mind. I thought about our previous disappointment and wondered how many times we could go through this before giving up. I made Josh answer. He said, "Mmm, okay, mmm, yeah," with no expression on his face. That did not tell me anything. I was getting impatient and wished I would have answered. Thankfully, my doubts were wrong. Lizzy just had to make a little change in plans, and we were all going to meet at Lizzy's house. My stomach settled some after I ate some of the warm cookies that my friend Kristen had dropped off for us. She knew I needed some warm sugar to calm my nerves.

The ride to Lizzy's house was long and quiet. We slowly pulled into the driveway, making sure it was the right house. It was a well-kept ranch house in a nice middle class neighborhood. Josh and I looked at each other before we got out of the car. *Well, here it goes*, I thought. As we walked the few steps from the driveway up a short sidewalk to the door, my heart raced, my palms were sweaty, and my mouth became dry. I heard the door open. I did not want to look up. There she was. She stood about 5'2" with straight blonde hair pulled back in a pony tail. She did not appear to be much younger than I was. When she smiled, her straight white teeth shined. I thought to myself, *Anyone would want her baby. Yet, she picked us*. I looked at Josh, and I could tell he was thinking the same thing. Lizzy immediately helped us feel at ease. She was at the door with a big grin on her face as if she had known us forever. She was beautiful with her high-pitched *hello* and her bubbly personality. Mallory was behind her. A tiny life was growing inside Lizzy's round belly. It was so exciting to see. She walked us into the living room, and we all sat down. Josh and I sat on a couch. Lizzy was in a lounge chair against a side wall. Mallory placed a chair where she could see us all and sat down.

Lizzy explained her reasons for choosing adoption. She shared many personal details, and we learned a lot about her that day. Lizzy explained how she knew right away that adoption would be the best option for this little baby. Lizzy and the birthfather were both in some very difficult circumstances.

They wanted their baby to have a better life than they could offer. They trusted God to find another family that could give this baby the home they could not provide. They had both made some bad decisions, and this was one decision they wanted to get right.

Lizzy had peace in knowing she was carrying this child for someone else. Mallory said that in twenty years of being a social worker, she had never seen someone so confident and unwavering in her adoption choice.

On January 29, 2008, I wrote in my journal: *We basically fell in love with the person she is. We are much alike and most of our views the same. The whole situation just seems too perfect and too good to be true…there are lots of prayers on both ends. I know He is hearing us. I truly just want His will and for Him to give us the strength and peace to deal with whatever that may be.*

After all, this woman was making a choice for a little life—one of the most difficult decisions she would ever have to make. And her decision could also affect us for a lifetime.

CHAPTER SEVEN

The Ultimate Phone Call

It was time for the waiting and guessing game again. *Did she like us? Was she going to choose the other family? Will she call us and when? Is this God's plan? Are we ready?* And it went on and on. Every time the phone would ring, my heart would pound and hit the walls of my chest with a thump. All of our friends and family were also waiting with excitement. We tried to continue on with our normal lives despite all of the anticipation.

Four days later, on Wednesday, January 30, 2008, at 12:14 p.m., I was at my friend Phoebe's house.

There were probably fifteen kids there. She had her kids, I had my kids, and we were both babysitting other kids. We were getting together to let the kids play. My cell phone rang. I wrestled with my purse to get it out in time. I saw it was Lizzy's number. Once again, the sinking stomach feeling hit me. The house was full of laughter, noise, and chaos. I took off running to the back of the house just so I could hear. When I answered, no one was there. "Oh, no! What do I do?" I said out loud. "Do I wait for her to call back? Did she call by accident? Oh forget it!" I could not take the wondering. I decided to call her back, and she answered right away. She told me that she had decided to pursue us as the adoptive parents. How does one respond to a comment like that? Try to imagine getting the call that you won something really big, something like the lottery but even better. This is a call that means that your life goals and dreams are coming true. It is a call that tells you that someone loves and trusts you enough to legally hand over a life that they love.

Lizzy sounded very happy. I think making a decision gave her some relief. I probably sounded like a bumbling idiot. We talked for a long time and discussed many details. She told me that she wanted us to be involved in everything. We discussed her next doctor's appointment. I was thrilled with the whole conversation. I called Josh right away at work. He told me he wanted to go out to eat and celebrate after he was off work. I was on the phone most of the day telling the whole world. Our family all met at Applebee's that night to celebrate. We received some of our first baby gifts at that dinner table.

I wanted to talk to Lizzy all of the time, but I did not want to drive her crazy. I thought about her and the baby constantly. *Is she sleeping okay? Is she eating well? Are there any signs of early labor?*

On February 7, we talked over the phone. We asked Lizzy if she had thought of any baby names. She said no, that she had just been calling her baby girl. She wanted us to name her. I told her that Josh and I had been discussing names. We liked the name

Grace because Lizzy told us in our first meeting that she has only been able to get through her hard times and carry this baby because of God's grace. The word *grace* and the name Grace meant so much to us also. We really wanted the name to be something that Lizzy liked, or at least did not hate. We liked the middle name Catherine because my mother and I were both named after my aunt Sara Catherine. Lizzy was happy. My mother, Mary Catherine, was very happy too! Lizzy told us that Grace was one of her three favorite names. She was very accepting of the name Catherine too. From that day on it was settled that baby girl was now Grace Catherine. In my Bible dictionary the definition of grace is: *God's free and unmerited favor for sinful humanity*. We did not yet know how well this name would fit.

We saw our first sonogram pictures of Grace later that day. Lizzy had sent them to us by e-mail. They were wonderful. I longed to have Grace close to us. I could not feel our daughter like Lizzy could, and I could not even be near her during this time. But tears rolled down my cheeks as I saw her form for the very first time. It made things seem real. There she was—Grace Catherine in all her glory in black and white fuzziness. She was so very small, yet so beautiful already.

CHAPTER EIGHT

Bumps in the Road

Time was passing. We had more conversations with Lizzy and grew closer in our relationships. Josh and I met with our lawyer, and Lizzy met with hers. Josh and I started working on turning the office into the baby's room. I had the urge to run out and buy pink, pink, and more pink. However, I still had that deep down fear of having to look at a pink room with no baby. I did not want to take that risk. After all, nothing is final until after the baby is born, and the papers are signed.

Journal entry February 7, 2008: *God, is your plan for us to be parents to Grace? Is it going to end up a disappointing test? Whatever it is Lord, may Your will be done and may You give us the strength we all need, whether good or bad, to endure with love, joy, and perseverance!*

I was not yet aware of the amount of strength and perseverance we were going to need in the very near future.

I went with Lizzy to our first doctor's appointment on February 27. Josh had to work, so he was not able to go. We were trying to save up some of his vacation days for Grace's arrival. Lizzy and I waited in the busy lobby for a long time. Lizzy likes to talk a lot like I do, so there were not many awkward silent moments. I wondered what some of the other people in the packed waiting room thought about us as they glanced our way. It probably didn't look too typical. My facial expressions of excitement and my tender hands moving around her protruding abdomen could not have been a common scene there. I sure did not witness anything else similar. Maybe they thought we were just sisters—who knows? We were able to learn a lot more about each other. I got to feel Grace kick and move around. This little one was not just kicking. I think she was doing some cartwheels and showing off for me. That was really cool. Lizzy said she was active all of the time.

Lizzy told me a little about her doctor, Dr. Ruby. Ironically, she was also an adoptive mother. I was glad to hear that. I felt it might give her more perspective on the whole situation. It can be awkward explaining why there are two moms in the room. Dr. Ruby had a little boy just like we did. His adorable pictures were hanging all over the office walls.

We finally got into the room. Lizzy introduced me to the staff as the adoptive mom. She seemed very comfortable and at ease with the whole situation. The doctor ordered a sonogram for the next day because Lizzy's abdomen was measuring larger than it should have. The doctor told us it could mean she was further along than we thought, there could be a problem, or everything could be fine. Josh and I both wanted to be there for that sonogram. Josh made some arrangements with work so he could go too.

The next day when Josh and I picked up Lizzy for the sonogram, she had been having contractions. When the doctor found out, she admitted Lizzy to the OB floor. So here we were—the three of us. We wheeled her over to admissions to check in. Josh and I just kept looking at each other, not knowing what to think or how to feel. It really was a little awkward. Throughout the admission process people asked who we were. Lizzy was very open and said, "These are the adoptive parents." She always said it in such a positive tone. That really helped us feel at ease and included. We felt like Grace's parents already, but we were not the ones going through the pain or making the decisions. All we could do was try our best to support and comfort Lizzy.

When Lizzy got to the OB floor, they gave her medications to stop the contractions and also gave her a steroid to help develop Grace's lungs in case they could not stop labor. Lizzy was only thirty weeks along, so all of this was pretty scary. All of the medical professionals told us they would do their best to stop labor.

The sonogram was awesome. Grace was playing with her toes. The sonographer said that she had never seen that before. Grace was already special. She was very active. We were all joking that she was running in there. She was the perfect size and appeared healthy. It was surreal getting to see her little face so clearly. There was our little girl.

After the sonogram they put Lizzy in a bed and started an IV. They were able to stop labor, so they let Lizzy go home on bed rest. Josh and I took her home that night. We had just been with Lizzy and knew things were okay, so we were not too worried. On Sunday morning we went to church. It was a great Sunday with the excitement of new life in the near future. When we walked out of church, I had two messages on my cell phone. I could not believe that I had turned my phone on silent. This was what I usually did on Sunday mornings, but circumstances were not the norm. What was I thinking? I should have at least put it on vibrate. Maybe God knew that we needed time with Him first. The messages were from Lizzy. In a quiet and calm voice she explained that she was having contractions again. She left a second message saying that a friend was taking her to the hospital. She was admitted to the OB floor again.

Josh and I rushed home to get a few things just in case Grace decided to arrive. My parents came to pick up Evan and take care of him. Evan was used to them picking him up on the spur of the moment, so he did not think anything of it. We rushed to the hospital. It took us about an hour to get there because it was several miles from home. We sat in the hospital room and talked with Lizzy as she and the baby were monitored. We learned some of the things that Lizzy liked to eat—dry cereal, maple donuts, and muffins. After all, food was something positive we could give her at that time. We wondered how long this could last. Would they be able to stop labor over and over?

That day was a little worrisome for other reasons also. There had been a flu outbreak. All of the staff were wearing face masks. One nurse said that she had never seen anything like it in her twenty years of nursing. There had been over eighty cases in that hospital in the last couple of days. They had to close the emergency room because they could not admit any more patients. It would be dangerous for Lizzy and the baby if she were to get the flu. And, if Josh or I were to get it, how would we be able to be there for Lizzy and keep juggling the rest of our lives? I prayed hard for God to keep us all healthy.

Josh and I stayed all day. We all learned more about each other. Labor was stopped again, but this time the doctor ordered complete bed rest. We took Lizzy home that night. It was really hard for me to leave her. I wanted to stay and take care of her and the baby. I knew we had a long way to go and that was not reasonable. I had a son, a home, and job to tend to. It was very difficult to know how to divide our time.

Even though we were not there with Lizzy and Grace daily, we still continued to stay in contact. It was very hard. We often felt helpless. We had been through so much with Lizzy already. We were becoming very close. She was having a hard time being on bed rest and unable to take care of herself. I think anyone in her situation would be depressed. At our next doctor's appointment the doctor told us that the goal was for the baby to make it to thirty-eight weeks gestation which meant seven more weeks. Lizzy cried when she heard, "Seven more weeks." I felt so sorry for her. There is no nice way to say this, but her belly was gigantic! It looked like there were a few babies in there. I couldn't imagine how she could make it another seven weeks.

On the same day, after the doctor's appointment, we went to lunch together. We talked about how we might be able to help get her through this. She had help from some of her friends, but none of her family lived near her. Lizzy and I talked at lunch that day about how we both knew that God must have a really special plan for Grace's life. We talked about how He brought us all together for Grace's sake.

I took her dirty laundry home; she was not allowed to be on her feet at all. Our families helped by sending food when they could. And, of course, we all prayed.

Journal entry March 5, 2008: *How exciting this all is! I know God's will and plan are busy at work. I feel it in the depths of my soul.*

One week later on March 12, it was time for the next doctor's appointment. Lizzy and I planned to go out after the appointment and do something fun. Lizzy was allowed to be in a wheelchair, and she was ready to get out of the house. When we got to the appointment, Lizzy's abdomen was measuring much larger than it should. The doctor ordered another sonogram right away. I could tell the doctor was more concerned than she was at our last visit. We went over to the hospital and had another sonogram done. Grace had her little hands clasped together as if she were praying. I think maybe God told her what was soon to come. The sonographer even wrote *praying?* on the picture.

The sonogram showed a large excess of amniotic fluid. The sonographer asked us to wait because she wanted to call the doctor. Next thing we knew, Lizzy was admitted to the hospital for the third time with this pregnancy, and the doctor ordered stress testing on the baby. We went back up to the very familiar OB floor for the third time. She was wheeled down the long blue-carpeted hallway back to the same room we had been in before. The rooms were spacious and pleasant with laminate wood floors. Curtains hung down the sides of the large windows. It was decorated like a home would be with pictures hanging on the walls. It set a comfortable environment for all of us. Most of the staff knew about us and our stories. Once again they put the large belt around Lizzy's belly to monitor the baby's movements and heart rate. It was another long day of hurry up and wait.

The results of the test showed that Grace had been in some distress. Because of this, Dr. Ruby ordered a transfer to a different hospital with a level 3 NICU. Dr. Ruby was not the type to push the panic button. She had a calm demeanor and spoke quietly. She was great with Lizzy, but a transfer was scary because Lizzy would not have her own doctors. She had been brave and strong all day, but this broke her down. Lizzy's tears started to flow. The doctor looked in my eyes and calmly recommended that Josh come to the hospital too. I felt a large lump in my throat and knew none of this could be good, but I also knew I had to be calm. It was late at night when the ambulance arrived. We both were exhausted and very scared for Lizzy and the baby. Lizzy was crying and asking me to not leave her side as the paramedics wheeled her out of the hospital room.

I rode silently in the front of the ambulance with the driver. It was awkward silence; he just looked forward and drove through the dark sleeping streets. We pulled into the garage at the new hospital. By this time it was after 10 p.m. The paramedics wheeled the gurney, with Lizzy strapped down, through the empty and quiet halls to the elevators. Everyone crammed in. There was one other woman in the elevator with us. She smiled and asked Lizzy how far along she was. She then explained to Lizzy that her little boy was upstairs in the NICU. She said he was born two weeks ago. He was born early at twenty-nine weeks but was doing very well. Lizzy was further along than that. Lizzy and I decided she was a human angel that God placed in our paths. Really—what are the chances that this woman would be going up late at night at the exact time that we were? The happy look on her face gave both Lizzy and me some hope and relief. And it was wonderful to know that her baby was going to be fine. It was like being able to take a breath after holding it all day long.

When we arrived at the hospital room, we were not sure what to expect. This room was not as welcoming as the other. It was much smaller with drab walls and white tile floor. One lounge chair was pinched between the bed and the wall. We were met by a perinatologist, Dr. Johns, with a sonogram machine. She was wearing gray-blue scrubs. She was a petite woman, shorter than Lizzy, with short, straight blonde hair and an intelligent look about her. Her face had a constant serious expression. I knew if this doctor was ready and waiting for us this late, it wasn't a good thing. Several staff moved Lizzy off the gurney and into her bed. The doctor did the sonogram herself. As she did it, I studied every move and facial expression trying to guess what it could mean. Dr. Johns moved the wand back and forth through the gel over Lizzy's stretched skin, and back and forth some more. Then she would click on the keyboard. The clicks echoed in the dark and quiet hospital room. She finally said that there was probably a birth defect causing the excess amniotic fluid. The heart was moved way over to the right side. She thought it might be a hole in the diaphragm, something fairly common that could be corrected by surgery. She said she wanted to do a more thorough sonogram on a better machine the first thing that next morning in her office. She also wanted to get the opinions of her partners.

When the doctor left the room, we just sat for a while. Josh decided to pick up Evan so they could both sleep at home. We decided I would stay with Lizzy. We listened to the continual thump, thump, thump of Grace's heart rate being monitored. Once in a while we heard an extra loud thump from Grace kicking. Lizzy moaned from pain and discomfort. She tossed and turned as well as she was able. The nurse had to come in often to readjust the monitor belt. I finally pulled up the footrest of the chair beside the bed so I could try to get a little rest, but Lizzy and I stayed up talking until 2:30 that morning. We could not sleep. I tried, but my mind was racing. So we laughed, cried, and prayed.

I woke early that morning feeling like my body was one large cramp from trying to sleep in a ball in the chair. Lizzy was still asleep, and I did not want to wake her. I went down the hall hoping to find a toothbrush, a restroom to wash my face, and a vending machine full of caffeine. Thank goodness someone knows what you need while in a hospital, because I found it all. I knew there was a chance that I might scare someone with my over-worn clothing, blood-shot eyes, and frizzed-out hair. So I had to at least brush my teeth so that I did not knock them over too. After all of that was taken care of, I went back into the room and waited while Lizzy slept.

Lizzy's glorious wheelchair ride arrived soon after. Josh got there just in time to go with us. They wheeled Lizzy down to the doctor's office as we followed behind. The transporter took us all into a room where the three of us sat in the dark waiting. The doctor entered. Dr. Lender was another perinatologist. He was tall with dark hair and probably middle-aged. He prepared the sonogram device, clicked for a while on the keyboard, and squirted the gel on Lizzy's large belly. Once again we watched closely as Dr. Lender moved the wand back and forth, back and forth. We looked for any sign that might give us a clue as to what was going on. Doctor Lender was also very serious with minimal expression. We began to ask a few questions. He seemed irritated and requested that we wait until he finished before asking questions. After a long period of silence he said, "This baby has a serious birth defect and may die." Silence fell upon the room.

"What? Die?" I said. "We thought this looked like a common and curable birth defect of the diaphragm."

As a dialysis nurse, I knew what it was like to get used to seeing serious illness. I also realized that all this doctor sees is problem pregnancies. But his response still felt cold. It felt as if he looked us right in the face with no expression, stabbed us in the heart, twisted the knife with all of his might, and then walked out the door.

As Dr. Lender was leaving, he said that he wanted both of his colleagues, two other perinatologists, to come and look also. The overhead lights were still off. Only a lamp's light shone. Lizzy was on the table; I was in a chair beside her, and Josh was in the chair beside me. I held Lizzy's hand and Josh held mine. We all squeezed hands. My hands were wet with sweat. No one spoke. The only sound was the sound of sniffles in the dark windowless room. Here we all were—hand in hand, waiting again.

The door soon cracked open, and the light peeked in. The doctor we had seen the night before, Dr. Johns, came in, along with another doctor who was a new face to us. The two doctors looked at the sonogram pictures on the television screen. They both gave their detailed opinions and then gave the same diagnosis before Dr. Lender even explained what he saw. It felt like they were talking as if we were not there, but I was really glad they were discussing things in front of us. I really did not want anything hidden—no false hopes. They all agreed that Grace had a severe and rare birth defect called CCAM type 3. We were so confused. All of the sonograms before yesterday had shown that Grace was perfect. How could this be? We were so scared and had many questions. They discussed everything in front of us, and they all seemed very confident. They came to this conclusion within minutes, so we knew they must be right. We squeezed each others' hands again. First the tears began to roll out, and then the sobbing came next.

The doctors began to explain the defect. It sounded a lot like blah, blah, blah, blah. After all, they had just told us our baby may die. What else is there to know? They explained that the left lung was actually one big mass of tissue that malformed. It was so big that it was pushing Grace's heart over and compressing her right lung. They said the good news was that the heart looked strong, even though it had a lot of pressure on it. Dr. Lender explained that the defect was no fault of anyone. It was not genetic, and there was nothing anyone could have done to stop it. He explained how amazing it is that so many babies come out normal. There are so many different tissues that have to grow in just the right places in just the right way. If one little tissue is not exactly right, then that organ will not grow correctly and do the job that it needs to.

We tried hard to take it all in. It reminded me of when I was in nursing school and I learned about fetal growth. It was a big thing that confirmed my personal belief in God. Everything has to be just right at just the right time. Every organ has its own special function. And, it all forms from two cells. A Creator's hand has to be involved in that.

The nurse, who happened to be named Grace, wheeled Lizzy out of the room. Josh and I followed. She was kind enough to lead us out the back door so no one had to see our tears and puffy eyes. Our hands were full of wet tissues. Our heads were tilted downward toward the white tile floor. We looked at tile after tile down the long hallways all the way back up to the hospital room. Soon after we arrived, Dr. Lender walked into the room. He handed us an article about Grace's condition that he had copied for us out of his medical book. I knew this was not very typical for a doctor. A doctor's time is always limited. Usually a doctor sends office staff, or a nurse if you are lucky, to deliver information. His expressions may have been flat, and his words all clinical, but I knew this was an act of sympathy for the whole situation. He did not say much at all; he just handed it over and went back to his work.

After Dr. Lender walked out the door, a neonatologist and a social worker walked into the room. You know it is never good when the social worker comes in with the doctor. The tall, thin, brown-haired doctor introduced herself. Softly, she said, "Hello. My name is Dr. Jenson."

She pulled a chair to the bedside and sat down. Lizzy was lying on the bed. I was sitting on the side of the bed beside her. Josh stood beside me. Dr. Jenson's eyes were on us, but her head was tilted down. She explained to us that a neonatologist is a doctor who cares for high-risk infants as soon as they are born. I could not believe how quickly she came to meet with us. I already knew things were bad, but then I knew they must be really bad. My heart began to thump so loudly I could hear it. She explained that she wanted to make sure we knew how severe this birth defect was. She said that she only sees it once or twice a year. All she sees are high-risk babies, and this hospital is where some of the most critical pregnancies in the city are admitted. Dr. Jenson said that she has seen infants survive a CCAM diagnosis. She also explained that Grace had the most severe type of CCAM which is type 3. She was kind and gentle, soft-spoken, and easy to listen to. She asked us if we had any questions, but we could not think of any. She just sat in the chair looking at all of us for a long time. I think she was waiting a while to see if we had any questions. She then told us that we needed to discuss plans for Grace if she did not make it. She actually used the words *funeral plans.* These were harsh words that we did not want to hear, but the doctor delivered them as gently as she could.

Dr. Jenson explained what it would be like the day Grace was born. With her eyes cast downward and a frown on her face, she explained that Grace was getting all of the oxygen she needed through the umbilical cord. At that time Grace was actually quite comfortable. But, when the umbilical cord was cut, Grace would have to breathe oxygen on her own. If the right lung, the good lung, was not made of normal lung tissue there would be nothing they could do for Grace. Grace would not be able to absorb oxygen on her own, and she needed oxygen to live. Even a ventilator would not help. There would be no chance of survival. If her right lung was made of normal lung tissue, they would still have the obstacle of the left lung compressing the right and not allowing it to expand. They would not know if the right lung was made of normal tissue until after delivery. Then, if Grace survived all of those complications, she would still have to survive a very major surgery to remove the mass that was pushing on the heart.

Dr. Jenson said the hospital would have a neonatal team present during the c-section. They would immediately put Grace on a respirator to help her breathe because of the lack of space on the right side. She said it would be good news if we heard her cry, but it would not necessarily be bad if we did not hear her cry. The team would take her immediately to the NICU. She explained that they may have to transfer Grace to Children's Health Hospital if needed. Mothers do not deliver there, so babies have to be transported. Children's Health is a level 4 NICU, the highest level of NICU available. She also explained that Children's Health is one of the few hospitals in the country that performs ECMO. This is a heart-lung bypass treatment used on critical infants. She explained that Grace would have to be at least thirty-four weeks to qualify for this treatment. She was now only at thirty-two weeks. She explained that Lizzy had excess amniotic fluid because Grace could not swallow it; her esophagus was pinched off from the mass. They were unsure if Lizzy would be able to make it to thirty-four weeks before delivering because of her uterus being too large.

Josh, Lizzy, and I tried to read the medical article Dr. Lender gave us after everyone left. Lizzy was frustrated. She threw it down and told us she did not understand any of it, and we would have to explain it. It was mostly medical terminology since it was out of a medical book. We were able to understand and explain the majority of it. But there were still some things that we did not understand. This was one of the few times when I wished I knew nothing about statistics and the medical field. I think it might have been better to have some false hope.

CHAPTER NINE

Searching for Hope

I had been strong for Lizzy through everything, but that night I broke down. I was exhausted, confused, and scared. Lizzy and I cried and cried. The nurses made her stay in one position most of the time. It was hard to track the baby's heartbeat because of the extra amniotic fluid. The nurses explained that Grace was swimming around in the large amount of fluid and could move from one side to the other very easily with all of the room she had. So it was hard to keep Grace on the monitor, and Lizzy had to constantly move and was never comfortable. She also continued to have contractions because her uterus was irritated from being so large. Lizzy was angry with her nurse and pretty much everyone else around her. She did not want any visitors or calls, but she wanted me to stay by her side. I felt as if I had a sister that I needed to take care of, and she just happened to be carrying our baby. It sounds very weird I know. It is one of those things where I think you have to be in that position to completely understand.

Josh was upset, yet appeared so strong at the same time. He is never the one to make phone calls. I tried to call a few people, but I could not do it without crying. I would talk myself through what I might say. I would get close to dialing the number, but I could not do it. Neither one of us wanted to call and tell our families the bad news. It was just one of those days. Lizzy and I were all cried out, and our eyes showed our exhaustion. I was still in the same clothes I had been in for two days—yuck!

Our nurse that day had no compassion despite our terrible news. She would simply come in to do necessary duties with few words and would move on. She kept telling Lizzy in an irritated voice that she needed to hold still for the monitor. The baby kept moving, and we would lose the heartbeat even when Lizzy did not move at all. Lizzy did not have much patience and told her nurse to get out! In addition to that issue, the hospital social worker was not very helpful when we asked questions. We felt we were a bother to her. This had been a problem since we had been there. I had given her the benefit of the doubt and thought she might come through when we needed her. Lizzy said she did not want her back in the room either. All of the doctors showed more compassion than these two staff. I wondered if maybe they were having bad days too. After all, they had personal lives outside of their jobs, and maybe their lives were as bad as ours. Our nurse apologized later, but that particular day we needed encouragement and patience rather than negativity.

I wanted to do something to help Lizzy feel better. So Lizzy and I prayed that God would send angels to guard the hospital room and keep out any evil. The prayer seemed to help. The next day the same social worker came to the door, but she did not enter the room. She just spoke a few simple comments to us from the threshold. After she walked away, Lizzy and I had a good laugh. We assumed the social worker had some negativity getting ready to come out of her mouth, and our angels kept her out.

During the quiet moments, I started thinking of so many things. *Will Grace live? Will she die? How will we cope? Will we ever want to try to adopt again? How will Lizzy cope? How would we plan a funeral? If she lives, how long will she have to be in the hospital and how much will she have to go through? What kind of life would that be for Grace? How will we afford months of medical bills? How will we be able to work and still spend time with Evan and time at the hospital? How will our family react? How can we let go of this dream? Why would all of this happen after we had been through so much?*

Mallory, our adoption social worker, met with me in the lobby that intense day after Josh had to leave for work. Josh had already used almost all of his vacation days, and we wanted to save a few for when Grace was born. It was horrible to have him leave that night, but we knew we would need his other vacation days soon. We also knew he had to work to keep our health insurance. Mallory and I sat on a small couch in the hospital lobby. Many people passed by. Other people were sitting in chairs near us. They were very likely going through difficult times also. I did not want to look up for others to see my red and swollen eyes. I would occasionally glance over to the right at the colorful stained glass on the chapel door; it was somewhat calming. Mallory and I quietly discussed the funeral. We also discussed the financial issues. She had many ideas and offered much support. She did more for us than I can explain. She went above and beyond for us. It was a big relief. She told me she would try to be at the hospital daily for support. She also told me that

I needed to go home and get some rest. Mallory was another human angel that God gave us. We had also talked with our lawyer that day about legal issues and medical insurance. The lawyer offered helpful advice too.

We had many advisors—lawyers, social workers, nurses, doctors, friends, and family. We were reminded by some hospital staff that there was nothing signed or legal yet, and that we did not have to go through with this adoption. A few other acquaintances questioned our decision, but Josh and I never had a second thought. We had already been through so much, and Grace was our baby no matter what the outcome. Our families gave us their full support and did not question our decision. We thought they might have some objections; but they not only agreed with us, they were by our side helping with everything they could and cheering us on.

I finally went home late that night and slept like I was dead. I woke up early the next morning, read my Bible, spent time in prayer, and felt refreshed to deal with whatever God had in store for us. I read in Lamentations about a new morning. "Because of the Lord's great love we are not consumed, for his compassions never fail. They are new every morning; great is your faithfulness. It is good to wait quietly for the salvation of the Lord" (Lamentations 3:22-23, 26). It was the perfect verse to read that day. It was a beautiful, sunny morning. I sat out on our screened porch, swinging back and forth, and looking at God's fingerprint on our world. The lake glistened. I could hear the swish of the wings of geese as they landed on the water. The grass was turning greener. I felt the warm sunshine on my face like a little ray of hope. I felt like I was ready to deal with the world again.

At the hospital our day went pretty well, but Lizzy and I both grew more tired as the day went on. It's amazing how quickly that refreshing morning began to slowly wear off. I picked up Evan in the afternoon and headed home. Late that night Josh came home from work, and my sister and Brian came over with pizza to cheer us up. Then my mom and dad stopped by. I was so glad to see them all. Our family gave me strength. I was ready to be refreshed again. We talked about everything and discussed plans for taking care of Evan while we were at the hospital. Even in a bad situation, I start to feel better coming up with a plan on how to deal with things. This helped, but the family was not in the best shape ever.

My sister, Stephanie, and I are very close and she was one of my big sources of support. We have always been there for each other. We usually talked every few days even when she lived far away. She was good at listening from her experience as a psychologist. But I really appreciated her advice and support as both my sister and as my best friend.

Stephanie had been very ill with bronchitis; her kids had been sick too. My mom and dad were leaving town for my mom's work, and she was stressed about passing all of her tests. Jann, my mother-in-law, had been spending time with her sister in the hospital. We had just received the news that our aunt's major surgery did not get all of her cancer. The day only seemed to bring more family difficulties.

The cold, dark, and rainy twilight seemed to be setting the scene for the rest of that night. Yes, there was more. My sister and her husband Brian, along with their kids, left our house around 12:00 a.m. They discovered that their family dog had been hit by a car in front of their house. Brian frantically called other family members to help bury the dog that night so the kids would not have to see her again. I called my sister and tried to calm her down, but I just did not have it in me—not an ounce, not a drop, nothing. I was physically and mentally exhausted. Josh left our house after midnight in the pouring rain to help them. I fell on my knees in sobs asking God, "Why, why, why, why?" I felt so much anger. I called my mom and let it all out. It was not pretty, and I said words I'd be embarrassed to repeat. I definitely messed up the part of the verse I had read earlier that says, "It is good to wait quietly." I felt like I had failed God and Satan had won that night. So much for the big, refreshing morning.

My sister was not only very sick, but now she was an emotional mess from the loss of her dog. It was a time when Josh and I needed to call in our support systems, but all of them already had full plates of their own. I told God that I could not take another thing. I asked, "God, why tonight, why now, why so much?" I was afraid for my parents to travel for fear that something might happen to them. *How were we going to get through this without our family's full support? How was I going to be there for them?* I wanted to put all of my loved ones in a protective bubble. I stood in our dark living room and sobbed so hard that I could not stand up. I felt as if I could not breathe. My legs became weak and I went to my knees, catching myself with the couch. I ended up in the perfect position to pray—which is where I needed to be—on my knees begging for more help, more refreshing. I felt so lonely. Everyone else in the family was trying to cope. Josh was gone. I knew

I had to get through this night on my own. As my breathing slowed and the tears went from pouring out to drips, I thought of a way to get through this.

I went upstairs to check on Evan as I do every night. I crawled into Evan's bed and held him; he was sound asleep. I could hear the rain hitting his window as the wind whistled. It was a soothing sound. I held little sleeping, limp Evan tightly in my arms. I squeezed him as more tears fell from my eyes onto his little freckled nose. I looked at his perfect four-year-old face; it looked so peaceful. I put his small, soft hand in mine. I thanked God that he was safe and in my arms. The spiritual warfare of that day shoved me into despair, and God used my sleeping son to pull me out.

It did not take much for the next day to be better than the previous, but it really was better. We were riding the rollercoaster of life. We went up, then down, then up again. It was Saturday. We did not make our usual daily trip to the hospital. Josh, Evan, and I spent the day resting together as a family. We spent a lot of time in prayer. I begged God to give us peace no matter what the outcome. It is hard to want His will, but He is the one who can see the future. We had already learned from the past that what might seem to be a tragedy at the time can later bring a lot of good. I thought of how it might be better for Grace to be with God if she would have to live on this earth with pain and many hospitalizations. I did not want her to suffer. I tried to think about what good could come out of a funeral for Grace. I thought of all the people that would gather together, many of whom do not see each other very often. Sadly enough, tragedy often brings people together. It also causes people to look to God for answers and strength. Maybe one person would be saved. I knew that was enough reason for God. I had vivid images in my mind of what the funeral might be like. I knew that God always has a better plan that we may never fully understand. I was willing at this time to accept His will, but I still felt a deep aching sorrow. I wanted Grace to live so badly. I wanted the dream of a baby girl to be fulfilled. But not just any baby girl—baby Grace. I wanted to hold her in my arms and bring her home to her family.

I began to think of the many people in the Bible who asked God for specific things. The Bible tells us that God wants us to enjoy our lives here on this earth. He wants to give us gifts. I thought about this because I really wanted this family. I thought of Hezekiah. "In those days Hezekiah became ill and was at the point of death. The prophet Isaiah son of Amoz went to him and said, 'This is what the Lord says: Put your house in order, because you are going to die; you will not recover.' Hezekiah turned his face to the wall and prayed to the Lord, 'Remember, O Lord, how I have walked before you faithfully and with wholehearted devotion and have done what is good in your eyes.' And Hezekiah wept bitterly. Before Isaiah had left the middle court, the word of the Lord came to him . . . 'This is what the Lord, the God of your father David, says: I have heard your prayer and seen your tears; I will heal you'" (2 Kings

20:1-5). God gave Hezekiah 15 more years to live. I know God knows everything, including our wishes and desires. But it seems in the story that Hezekiah changed the way God responded just by revealing his desires in prayer.

I was sure that God knew we wanted Grace to live, but I decided we would talk to God about what we were really thinking and what we really wanted. From that moment on we changed our prayers.

Journal entry March 16, 2008: *So I asked God if there is any way that He could save Grace, give her a happy and healthy life, and still do His will, to please, please do it.*

It was this same day that I realized how often we had gotten together to mourn. We had had three funerals of three close family members on my side of the family in just the past three years; two were tragic. That is too much mourning if you ask me. How often do we get together to celebrate? Yes, we do celebrate birthdays and holidays. But how often do we get together and celebrate when something wonderful happens? Do we celebrate God when life happens in the same way that we mourn when death happens? Does a miracle bring a family together in the same way that death does? I pondered all of these things. I think the answers are no and no again.

If we promised God we would bring people together in His honor, maybe He would change our path also. Second journal entry March 16, 2008: *We could have a praise service or celebration service. Why can we not get together to celebrate and say thank you to God and others for His miracles?*

As I thought of this, I felt peace once again. I talked with Josh about all of my thoughts. He agreed with everything.

That evening my parents came by. Mom came bearing gifts for Evan, and chocolate and snacks for Josh and me. Our bedroom seemed to be our main gathering place for relaxing. It was dark out, and our lamps gave the room a dim light. Evan and Mom were giggling and playing on the floor with the transformers she had brought him. Dad plopped himself on the bed beside me and put his arm around me as he shoved the chocolate in his mouth that my mom had brought for me. My dad can eat chocolate anytime. Chocolate is a comfort food for me also. It must be genetic. We were all comfortable and glad for a little rest. I began to tell my dad about all of my thoughts from the day. I asked him what he thought about how I changed my prayers. When it comes to the Bible and spiritual things, my dad, Steve, is my go-to man. He was a full-time pastor for twenty years and continues to preach when he can. He has a master's degree in divinity and a doctorate in ministry. He is a retired chaplain from the Army National Guard. He is a Christian counselor and owns his own counseling center. Besides all of that, he lives what he preaches and has a close connection with the Father upstairs. He agreed with the prayer, nodded with an approving smile, and said that is what we would all start praying for. He also liked the celebration service idea. He explained that maybe God wanted us to completely give in to His will so that we could have peace about whatever happens. I think Dad was right. Of course, behind most good men is a good woman. I looked over at mom and got the nod from her too.

Third journal entry March 16, 2008: *I do not have any strong feelings one way or the other about what might happen. But I know that Grace has hundreds, if not thousands, of people praying. Our church, our family and their churches, friends and their churches, co-workers, birth family and their churches—they are all praying for us! It is amazing!*

"Do not be anxious about anything, but in everything, by prayer and petition" (Philippians 4:6). "Therefore confess your sins to each other and pray for each other so that you may be healed" (James 5:16).

Many of our friends and family showered us with gifts, support, prayer, and love. Family issues were settling, and our family began to step in along with everyone else we knew. Jann, my mother-in-law, went to be with Lizzy in the hospital so I would know

Lizzy was not alone and I could spend a day with Evan. Jann brought Easter baskets filled with candy. Once again, chocolate can always help the day get a little better. Mallory spent a day with Lizzy in the hospital. She brought us ice cream and candy. Later that night my good friend Phoebe brought cupcakes and gifts to the house. She knows me too well. As much as I do not want to admit it, I did eat the cupcakes in addition to all of the other treats I already had that day. I am sure there was excess sugar running through my veins for days.

Mallory knew a woman named Mary that she calls her second daughter. Mary happened to be a NICU nurse at the hospital where Lizzy was staying. She had been visiting Lizzy and praying with her. Mary talked with us about Grace's condition in detail and what we might expect once she is born. Having her to talk to and having her visit Lizzy was a great relief. Mary was able to provide company and support for Lizzy numerous times. She was yet another blessing and an angel to us.

On March 17, Josh and I arrived at the hospital. The doctor performed a sonogram in the room. Grace had no hydrops, which is fluid around the heart or lungs. Hydrops could have made an already severe condition even worse. This was good news. We knew with each sonogram that this was something we did not want them to find. They also told us that both Josh and I would be allowed in the OR with Lizzy for the c-section. The hospital had informed us earlier that they allowed only one extra person in the OR. I did not want Josh to be out in the hall waiting alone. I wanted to be there for Lizzy, but I wanted Josh and me to be together. So this was great news!

On March 19, another sonogram was done. Dr. Lender said that the bad lung had shown some improvement. He made the comment that the baby just might come out and shock us all. He said that the heart was still shifted but was beating strong. He said that the longer Grace could stay in the womb and grow stronger, the better her chances were. He reminded us that medicine is never one hundred percent. I know that is completely true, but it was nice to hear those words of reassurance. The same doctor then pointed to Lizzy's Bible and told her to keep reading. That moment struck me. For some reason I was surprised; however, I was thankful to have a doctor at least acknowledge the Bible as a good book to read. In another journal entry I wrote: *There are so many people praying for baby Grace. I think God might be handing out one of his miracles. Lizzy was feeling better and looked better too. I was so excited to share with everyone the good events of the day that I had been pacing the floor. I sent out a text to almost every phone number in my phone. It felt so great to finally send out some positive news.* Even though this was a small amount of hope, it was still hope.

CHAPTER TEN

Hope Falls

On Thursday, March 20, 2008, I arrived at the hospital in the morning. Lizzy was extremely swollen. She told me that the morning's sonogram showed her amniotic fluid level had greatly increased. She was having very painful contractions. Her blood pressure was high and there was protein in her urine. She had rapidly declined over one day's time.

Here went the life rollercoaster down a very steep hill. I was worried about her and the baby. Grace was only thirty-three weeks and three days, not old enough to receive ECMO if she needed it. I was also worried about Lizzy's health. The doctor walked in soon after I arrived and said, "We are taking the baby at 7:30 a.m. tomorrow. We have to look out for baby and mom, and we cannot wait any longer."

Lizzy, bless her heart, was blown up like a balloon and in constant pain and discomfort. She looked at the doctor and told him "No, I can make it longer." Dr. Lender explained to her why that was not an option.

Shortly after Dr. Lender left, a neonatologist and his team entered the room. The doctor had kind eyes. He appeared to be in his thirties. Dr. Jolley introduced himself and his team. He came in with a sad look. He calmly explained that they would all be in the room for Grace's birth. He reminded us that this was a severe situation and that we could lose the baby. Hearing those words again—*lose the baby*—brought all of the anxiety back. I had lost so much fear just a day ago. Things were positive and our hope was restored. My anxiety was melting away. Now those five simple words, *we could lose the baby*, broke the dam of my river of fears. Fear rushed through my body. Hope crashed. Here was all of the bad news again. I felt my face flushed, and the lump in my throat kept growing larger and larger. I choked back the tears so that Lizzy would not see my fear. Lizzy trusted my opinions and advice. I had to stay strong for her.

I stayed calm outwardly as thoughts rushed through my mind that this was it. Dr. Jolley explained how they would intubate Grace immediately after birth, and there would be a full neonatal team to take care of her. As soon as they finished talking, I excused myself to the hallway. I leaned against the railing in the hallway as it felt like all of my strength was leaving my body. I held my head down so no one could see me. The waiting room was full, so there was no private place. The neonatal team and all of the nurses were whispering at the nurses' station. I had my back to them, but I could see them out of the corner of my eye. They were only about twenty feet behind me. It was one of those times in life when people are all around, yet you feel so alone. I wanted and needed my family to soothe the pain and fear. I longed for Josh to be there, to hold me up, and tell me it would all be okay. I did not want anyone to hear me sob, so I kept holding back, but my tears still poured out and splattered on the hard tile floor. I knew I had to gain my composure and be there for Lizzy. She seemed strong—maybe even relieved that this would soon be over.

I gathered my composure and went back into the room. I asked Lizzy who she wanted me to call. I took the list and went into a little corner of the crowded waiting room down the hall. I had spent a lot of time alone in that waiting room, so I was comfortable there. I went down the phone number list which took a while. The next thing I knew, I felt someone standing behind me. It was Lizzy. She was standing there in the crowded waiting room in her extra-large men's t-shirt; nothing else fit. She had no monitors on, and she was not accompanied by any medical staff. She said softly, "I do not want to be alone."

I was in shock. In my best sister and nurse mode I yelled, "Whaaaaaat are you doing?" Without saying anything else I got up. Lizzy waddled back to the hospital room, and I was by her side. I scolded her for getting out of bed, but then we laughed about it. I told her I would not let her be alone.

While sitting with Lizzy, I didn't know which emotion to let take over. I wanted to be excited. Our baby was going to be born tomorrow! A new baby girl! But then I wondered if we would we be there to witness her first and last breath. *Would we have to hand her right back to God?*

I called Josh at work right away. He left work to pick up Evan and head for home. I called my sister, and she left work right away to come be with me at the hospital. Some of Lizzy's friends came. One of her friends, yet another angel, came to spend the night with her so I could go home. We did not want to leave Lizzy that night, and she did not want to be alone. But we had to go home to pack and prepare to stay in another state for adoption legal purposes. It was hard to know what to pack. We knew we could be staying an hour's drive away from our home for up to two weeks. We all prayed over Grace that night with our hands on Lizzy's belly—five women. My sister was amazed because Grace kept kicking everyone. I think she was giving high fives for the prayers. She wanted us to know she was there.

Thankfully, my mom and dad had just arrived home. They were on their way into town when we called with the news. They helped us talk through some plans. They agreed to pick up Evan that night and keep him with them. We did not tell Evan everything that was going on. We felt it would be too much for a four-year-old to understand. It was hard enough to understand as an adult. When my parents arrived at our house late that night, we squeezed Evan and gave him kisses, telling him good-bye for an unknown period of time. I was thankful that he did not have to deal with all of the questions and anxiety in his little mind, but I was afraid of how we would need to explain things the next day. After they left, we did our best to pack for ourselves and for baby Grace. I cannot remember what we packed. I do know we had clean clothes. I also remember trying to decide what to do with the video camera. We did not want to miss the opportunity to have the birth of our daughter on video. But how would we cope if we had a video of her last breath. We decided to take the chance, and we packed it.

CHAPTER ELEVEN

The Big Day

We arrived at the hospital the next morning by 6:00 a.m. and walked into that familiar hospital room for the last time. By this time Lizzy looked like a pencil with a grapefruit stuck in the middle, but she seemed to be doing really well. I told her that her faith was much stronger than mine. She just kept saying that she knew Grace was going to be okay.

Randy, a family friend and a minister, prayed with everyone. Some of Lizzy's friends and family were there as well as all of our family. Mary, the

NICU nurse, came up on her day off to sit with our family and answer any questions they might have while they waited.

The morning went by fast. The surgical team entered the room and told us to put on our blue gowns, caps, and booties. The nerves set in quickly. My stomach was burning. Lizzy was shaking. As hospital staff wheeled her down the long hallway in the bed, I walked alongside holding her hand. Josh trailed not far behind. I kept praying over and over for God to fill our room and take Grace in his hands. I had been praying for God to just give us one cry so we would know if she was going to be okay.

Now we are back in the cold, bright operating room when I felt as if my heart stopped beating. I heard more booties swishing across the floor. Lizzy's sweating hand clasped tightly around mine. I glanced over at my husband and looked into his concerned eyes. Then I peeked over the blue drape that was across Lizzy's chest. I saw Grace's head. Then I heard it—two loud cries! Not just one, but two! It was the sound I longed to hear. It was like music. I knew Grace had to have some working lung space to be able to cry. I knew we had a little hope. She arrived at 8:01 a.m. on that Good Friday morning. The neonatal team quickly grabbed her and cut the cord. They all huddled over her, working and counting the seconds out loud. We could barely see her. There was no time to show her to us. It was really hard to tell what was going on only five feet from us. But we had to stay back and wait. They were not telling us what was happening at this point, but it was obvious that things were intense.

We just stood still and watched as we knew we had to. Several specialized medical workers focused on one new little life, hovering over her and working swiftly. We could not tell if she was breathing on her own. By the time we could see her, she had a tube in her mouth. We had the video camera on during the whole event and captured Grace's two magnificent cries. We were only in the OR for about thirty minutes. Then the neonatal team quickly wheeled Grace out of the OR to the NICU. Josh and I were allowed to follow. As we passed the waiting room full of our family and friends, I yelled, "She cried!" Everyone knew what this meant. They all screamed and cried. I actually saw some of them jumping up and down; seeing adults with their feet off the ground was quite a sight! We went into the elevator and up to the NICU. Lizzy's friend stayed with her. We had to stop at the nurses' desk to fill out a few health risk forms. Then we scrubbed in at the large stainless steel sink for the very first time. A nurse came over to give us instructions and gave me a blue gown and gloves. I had to gown up since I was a health care worker and more likely to carry illness due to exposure.

As we were allowed back into the NICU, we got a better look at Grace. The medical staff had placed a lot of tubes and lines in her. They had her hands and feet tied down so she would not move too much. The staff used medications to get her stabilized. Two nurses worked continually on her and did not leave her side. Grace was on a high frequency ventilator, called an oscillator, on the highest setting to keep oxygen in her blood. It vibrated and shook her whole, tiny, fragile body. Dr. Jolley told us that because they were already doing everything they could, they would not be able to do anything for her if her condition began to decline. He reminded us that babies this critical can decline very quickly. At this point Dr. Jolley was pleased that she was here. He explained to us that she was still very critical, but she was critically stable if that made sense. It made sense to us.

When everything settled down a little and most of the medical staff stepped back, we were able to take a breath and look at our new, beautiful baby, Grace Catherine. We just stood and stared at her while everyone worked on her. I was able to hold her tiny little hand. I looked over my new baby girl, and she was much like I had imagined. Her scant amount of hair had a strawberry tint. Her skin was a pale pink. Her eyes were swollen and closed. Her fingers and toes were long and skinny. Her little ears, lips, and nose looked just like a baby doll. Despite the strong vibrations she looked peaceful. The doctor came by often to check on us.

Dr. Jolley was wonderful. He explained everything as best he could. He asked us to follow him so he could show us her first chest x-ray. He led us through the hallway into a room nearby. It was a small, gray room with no windows; it was just big enough to fit a desk and a few chairs. He pulled up two chairs to the desk. He stood behind us and offered us a Jolly Rancher from the jar of candy sitting on the desk near a computer screen. There was another doctor standing behind him. He showed us Grace's first chest x-ray and its abnormalities. We had been told we would know more about her condition and its severity once she was born and we could get an x-ray. An x-ray is a much better picture than a sonogram done from outside the womb. Josh and I both stared intently, trying to understand what we were viewing. We saw a lot of black and white, and nothing looked much like the typical chest x-rays that I was used to. He began to explain the x-ray to us. The lung appeared to be a large mass, and the heart was still shifted over. A tiny area of open lung tissue was on the right side. This much was obvious to me. While we were still in this room, he told us that he had called Children's Health Hospital with a report and requested a critical care transport. The current hospital had a NICU transport team, but they did not have the specialized equipment that Children's Health Hospital had.

Dr. Jolley stayed close by us until the transport team came a few hours later. At one point, while he was talking with us, his face got a little red, his eyes watery, and he said, "I really give you guys kudos for what you are doing. Most families would not have stuck it out. This really tells me a lot about your character and who you are."

I could only think about how we were the blessed ones, getting a chance to be parents of this little life. It felt nice to get such a compliment and not feel like the odd people hanging around who have no legal rights. I often wondered through all of this if people saw us as the intruders or as the parents. These comments helped us feel like we were already accepted as Grace's parents. As Dr. Jolley complimented us, I thought about what kind of man he had to be in order to do his job and do it so well. He worked in a level 3 NICU with critical and hurting babies, scared families, and hormonal mothers. And he did it day after day. Now that deserved some kudos. I could not hold back the urge and gave him a great big squeeze-type of hug! Josh laughed at me. I wanted to tell him how great I thought he was, but the words were not there. The crazy woman hug expressed it all. I could not help myself.

Before we left, he said good-bye and called us stellar. "So he thinks we are stellar!" I said to Josh. "What do you think he means by that?"

Josh laughed at me lovingly, like he often does. "He means that we're being strong," said Josh. We did not tell Dr. Jolley at that time that our strength came from God and our family.

As we waited for the critical transport team, we brought our family members back one by one to meet Grace for the first time. It was not a quick and easy task. Only one person could go at a time, and Josh or I had to be present, so we took turns. We had to decide who would get to go in first and in what order—and we did not want to hurt anyone's feelings in the process. It's silly how you can still worry about these things in the midst of a crisis, but everyone was chomping at the bit to get back there.

The grandparents went first—Maw Maw Mary, Paw Paw Steve, Minny Jann, and Pa Pa Bob. My sister, Stephanie, and sister-in-law Rachel were next, then my brother-in-law Brian. It was quite a process! First we met them in the waiting room; then they had to fill out forms at the NICU front desk, then they scrubbed and scrubbed and scrubbed at the sink, they walked down the hall, and then, finally—behold—Grace. I couldn't wait to show her to everyone. I just wanted to hold her up and announce to the world she was here, but those NICU nurses might have hurt me!

With each family member that visited Grace, I could see joy and sadness mixed together. Grace was here and she was beautiful, but she was being kept alive by tubes and machines. I could tell it was overwhelming for everyone. No one really knew what to say.

After all of the visits were over, I pulled up a tall stool next to tiny little Grace. I was wearing my full blue gown and blue gloves as I touched her small shaking hand. I wanted so badly to touch her skin. I wanted to pick her up and feel her life and warmth against me. But I couldn't because of her condition. I was thankful to feel the warmth of her tiny hand through my thick rubber glove. This was the calmest moment of the day.

The family went down to the cafeteria to eat. Josh and I stood and waited for the transport team while we watched our little girl sleep. While sitting on the tall stool, with my one gloved finger wrapped in Grace's hand, I began to nod and fall asleep. The last few hours had been filled with noise and chaos. It was finally calm and quiet. Grace was alive, and that moment was one of rest and peace.

The Children's Health Critical Transport Team arrived with all of their equipment. There were four on the team. They wore matching colors and appeared so professional. Each one of them had a different job. One of them, named Chris, took the time to explain every detail while the others worked on Grace. His slow, southern drawl was soothing. He asked if we had any questions. I think I just stood there in la-la land. It was not like me to not ask questions. I am typically the inquisitive one, especially when it's related to the medical field. But this was beyond me, so I trusted them. They were thorough and kind. They helped me feel more comfortable letting Grace out of our sight and into the hands of complete strangers. It took over thirty minutes to move Grace from all of her equipment to theirs. They had to give her many medications to stabilize her. She didn't seem to be in pain, even though the oscillator shook her chest and the rest of her body continuously.

After some hard work, she was completely moved to their isolette—a plastic enclosed bed. It was time to go. The transport team quickly rolled Grace down to Lizzy's room so that Lizzy could see Grace before she was transported. They let Lizzy touch her hand for one minute. Lizzy smiled and said thank you to the team. We made sure Lizzy was okay and was being taken care of. Her friend was staying with her.

The team explained to us what it would be like when Grace arrived at Children's Health Hospital. The drive would take about thirty minutes. They said we would not be allowed to see her for an hour after we arrived. The staff had to assess her and get her situated in her new place in the NICU. Then the team rolled Grace through the hallway to an exit where the ambulance was waiting. We nervously departed from Grace and the transport team and headed down the hallway to leave for Children's Health Hospital.

As we were exiting the OB unit, a nurse stopped us. Our social worker from the hospital called the nurses' station and asked the staff to find me and

Josh. She told us that Lizzy had to write a notarized release for us to be able to be with Grace. We panicked. Thoughts raced through my mind. *Are you kidding? We are on our way out the door to be with our critical baby who has no one else to be with her! Are you telling us we cannot go because of legal reasons? What if she dies alone? I cannot believe this!* (Insert some of the worst words you can think of here. That is what was in my head.) We had no doubt we were going to be loving and raising this child for the next eighteen years and for the rest of our lives, and we were not allowed to be with her? Screw the legal system! Sorry, those were my thoughts at that moment. I know the nurse could see the complete panic on both of our faces.

The nurses made many phone calls and quickly dialed number after number trying to reach a social worker and a notary. They could find neither in the entire hospital. They even tried to call other hospitals. I guess that is what happens when it is the Friday before a holiday. How would we get this done on Easter weekend if we could not get it done today? We were stuck. But we refused to believe that we could not be with Grace all weekend. We paced in front of the nurses' station. I kept saying to myself, "Think, think, think; there has to be some kind of solution. Please, God, help us!"

We called Mallory, our adoption social worker. She didn't answer, so we left a message. She finally called back and said Children's Health Hospital would approve a note of permission from Lizzy with a double witness signature—whew! Thank God for Mallory being available at that moment. That was a close call right before the holiday weekend.

When we told Lizzy about this, she frowned and said, "Whatever we have to do, let's do it. I don't want Grace alone!" Lizzy signed the papers, and we moved our feet as fast as we could down the long hallways and out the door to our car. The drive was long. We wondered what they were doing to Grace and how long we would have to wait to see our new little girl.

We finally arrived downtown at Children's Health Hospital. We drove several levels down through the underground garage. We rode the elevator up to the main entrance. We had to stand in line to have our driver's licenses scanned and put on our name badges to get into the hospital. Then we followed the signs pointing toward the NICU. We went up several floors and through several hallways. We reached the front desk of the NICU and signed in. I was afraid we would have to deal with the fact that we were not legal guardians. I eagerly showed them our bracelets that we wore at the other hospital with Grace's name and information. I knew this would help our cause. I also knew I did not plan on taking that bracelet off for a long time just in case anyone gave us any trouble. They gave us our "parents" name badges. That was a relief. It said *parent*. It did not say *wanna be parent* or *not legal yet* or anything obnoxious like that.

The staff informed us that they were waiting for us, and Grace was already situated. We could go back and see her—we were so happy! It had not quite been an hour. The secretary touched a button and the locked double doors swung open, inviting us in. A staff member walked us into the scrub room. It was a small room with about ten lockers in it for families. A very wide and deep steel sink allowed two or three people to scrub in at the same time. Posted signs told us how to use the sponge on our arms up to our elbows. A fingernail scrubber was on the other side. A short line of parents waited outside the door to scrub in.

The staff member pointed out Grace's station. She was not very far—about thirty feet straight ahead. We could see her tiny shaking body at the end of her pod as we walked toward her. We looked over the area. It was a large room with many walls dividing the room. When we walked between two walls, four sections separated by curtains were along each wall. This was a pod. Most of the time the curtains were all open so it looked more like eight babies in one big room. A hand-washing island was right in the middle of the pod. The floor was covered with colorful carpet down the middle of the pod and decorative tile on each station floor. The walls were bright and multicolored. Everything looked clean, tidy, and controlled. Each baby's station had a vinyl lounge chair or two and whatever equipment the babies needed. Each station looked different because all of the babies' needs were different. Some stations had isolettes, some little cribs, and some big cribs. There were some ventilators and a variety of other interesting equipment. It was quieter than most hospital units, even though there were over sixty babies in this unit.

We quickly arrived at Grace's station. Despite all of her lines and tubes, she looked peaceful in her small bed. Two RN's were continuously assigned to Grace. They introduced themselves in a whisper and explained a few things to us as they continued to work. They were watching her monitor very closely. One nurse explained how we could touch her head, hands, or feet. We were not supposed to rub her or be too loud because too much stimulation can be very irritating for preemies with their underdeveloped nervous systems. They did not make me wear gloves, and I was able to touch her soft, warm skin for the very first time. I placed my finger in her palm and let all of her fingers encircle my one finger. It felt so good.

The new doctors were still calling Grace *critical.* After we spent some time with Grace, we were able to bring some of the family to see her. They were all waiting patiently in the full waiting room. Just like the other NICU, only one visitor was allowed back at a time, and that person had to be with me or Josh. We went through the same process. Bring the person back, scrub in, visit Grace, and then call the next person. After all of the visitors left, we spent some time sitting quietly with Grace. It was getting late, and we knew someone needed to pick up Evan.

Evan had been with Phoebe all day. My sister's friend Amy kept my sister's two kids all day even though they were both running fevers. What a friend! My parents picked up Evan to keep him overnight so we could go back to the hospital the next day. Many people had done what they could to help us get through the past several months so we could make it to Grace's birth day. It took even more to get us through that single day. Grace was alive, Lizzy was doing well, and we were surrounded by loving family and friends. I think that was a good way to end an extra-special Good Friday.

I was not sure we would be able to sleep that night. After all, I had been having many sleepless nights. High emotions seem to be far more draining than any physical workout. This day was definitely packed full of a variety of emotions—fear, anxiety, irritation, love, joy, happiness, and rejoicing. It seemed these were all fitting emotions for an Easter weekend. Despite the high emotions, Josh and I both slept well once we arrived home. I think it was because Grace was finally here, she was alive, and she was getting great care.

CHAPTER TWELVE

Learning the NICU Life

A new morning brought a new way of life. Josh and I woke up refreshed and headed toward the hospital. After the typical entry process, we were at Grace's side. When we arrived, the medical team saw us and came over to talk with us. The medical team consisted of the doctor, nurse practitioner, and RN. Sometimes a social worker, dietician, and/or respiratory therapist was with them. Everything they told us was encouraging. There were some very small improvements, but we looked at even small improvements as something positive. The medical team planned to slowly wean her down on the oscillator settings. This was good news to us. We knew if she no longer required the highest setting, then we could always increase the setting if she started to have any kind of difficulty.

Grace had two umbilical lines. One line was used for arterial blood gas draws every four hours. Those results determined the oscillator settings. The other line was to give her total parenteral nutrition, also know as TPN. This was nutrition that went directly into her bloodstream instead of through the stomach. She had three EKG leads to monitor her heart. She had a half-dollar sized gold heart sticker stuck to her stomach that had a cord to the warmer. The warmer automatically adjusted its settings according to Grace's body temperature. She had a brown wrap around her foot with a glowing red light to measure her oxygen saturation. She had the ventilator tubes and a suction tube down her throat and taped to her cheeks. She had three medication pumps. One pump supplied proteins, and one supplied dopamine to keep her blood pressure up. The third pump administered ampicillin and gentamicin because of the ventilator and a possible infection. She also received morphine and Versed to keep her calm and to keep her from fighting the ventilator tubes.

Even with all of this medical mess, her little limp body still looked beautiful. We spent the day getting to know our daughter. We lightly placed our hands on her head, hands, and feet. We watched as the machine breathed for her. We talked about her future and the life that she may have ahead of her. We decided things were stable enough that it was time to tell big brother all about his new little sister.

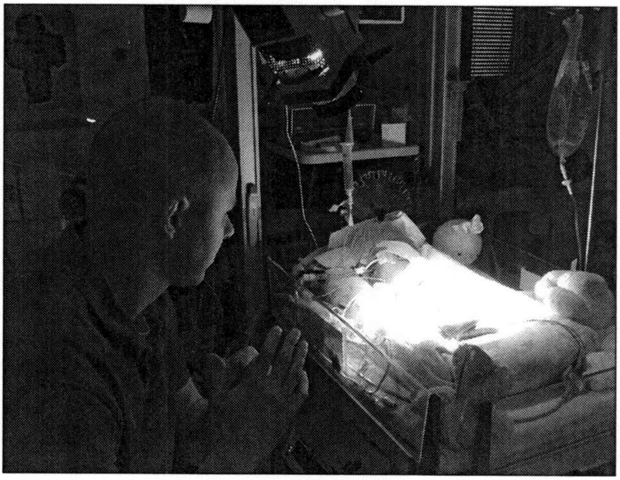

We left the hospital that night and went to Josh's work to develop our pictures. We also picked up eggs and dye so we could decorate Easter eggs with Evan. This was one of his favorite traditions, and we wanted to do something a little special with him. After our pictures were ready, we showed Josh's co-workers our first pictures of baby Grace. With some hesitation everyone "oooed" and "awed." We were both very proud. We bought some little photo books that we could put pictures in to give to Evan and our nieces and nephews, since they would not be able to meet Grace for a while. Kids were not allowed in the NICU because there were so many cases of influenza going around. If an already fragile baby caught influenza, it would not be a good prognosis. We thought the books would help the kids feel included.

After we left the store, we arrived at my parents' house. We told Evan about Grace on a four-year-old level. We told him that he had a new sister, but he would not be able to see her for a little while because she was sick. We showed him the pictures and let him choose some to put in his book. He smiled at us and started thumbing through the pictures. He took his time placing each one in his new book. I held him in my arms while he asked questions about the pictures. He did not seem to need much explanation. After arriving home at 10 p.m., we painted Easter eggs. Evan made a pink egg for Grace with her name on it written in crayon. Then we put him to bed so the Easter bunny would not go past our house. I called the night nurse to check on Grace three times during the night. The hospital staff were always kind and encouraged our calls.

Easter Sunday was a wonderful day. We were thankful that Grace was alive and receiving such great care. We got to spend time with Evan. We had been missing him so much! Evan wanted to wear his new big brother shirt to all of our Easter events. He carried his pictures with him all day. He liked to point out to others that Grace had a vagina, which meant she was a girl. I tried not to be embarrassed since he was so serious and proud. He often asked how many days and minutes until he could see her. It was hard for us to tell him that we did not know. He made up a song for Grace, and we taped it to play for her. Easter is my favorite holiday, but this one was extra special. During the Easter sermon my eyes kept filling up with tears. The warm sun rays filled the sanctuary, a promise of spring and new life. My family was there with us, and I could feel God's love and comfort. We were so full of hope, love, and life. We were parents again! We had a baby girl! Our pastor shared with the congregation our joys and concerns. Grace was a big part of Pastor Dave's special Easter prayer.

After church we went to my parents' house for Easter lunch and our annual Easter egg hunt. Josh's family joined us. The sun was still shining brightly. The kids giggled as they ran through the yard searching for eggs full of candy and prizes. We shared some laughter and tears with our family. We enjoyed the "ginormous" spread of home cooked food, but soon became anxious to make our rounds and get to the hospitals.

We decided to visit Lizzy first and bring her some Easter lunch. It was hard when we saw her. I felt bad for her being in the hospital on Easter. When we arrived, she said that she had been missing us. We gave her some food and a little Easter basket that we had put together. Thank goodness some of her friends had been there. Her mother had to go back home; I was really disappointed about that. I was hoping she would be able to stay with her for a while. That had been the plan. I was still concerned about Lizzy's health, especially since her blood pressure was still high. She said she was disappointed that she did not get to hold Grace. The plan, before we knew there were problems, was that we would hold the baby first and then Lizzy would hold her. We gave Lizzy some pictures of Grace and assured her that she would get to hold Grace as soon as the doctors would allow it. She hugged us both and cried. "Thank you," she said through her tears. After being with Lizzy through everything, it was hard to leave. Juggling our time between Evan, Grace, and Lizzy was exhausting. There just wasn't enough time to do it all. Eating and sleeping seemed to be on the back burner. We could do neither of those things while we were in the NICU.

We spent the rest of that Easter Day—day three—with Grace. She was still showing some slight improvements. The respiratory therapist had been able to turn down her oscillator settings a bit more. Everything else was mostly the same. Josh and I got to spend five hours sitting together in quiet, something we rarely did. Many of the babies had their stations decorated with items to fit their own little personalities. Some of the stations were decorated by the nurses, and others were done by the family. Grace had a big, white dry-erase board behind her raised bed. Her bed was about two feet wide by three feet long, and three and a half feet tall. Six inches of clear plastic wrapped around the bed. We hung up pictures that the kids of our family and friends had made for her. We put pink bows and flower stickers all around. We posted Bible verses printed in pink by her bed to remind ourselves and others of God's amazing love for this baby girl. After all, if this was going to be a long journey, we wanted to make it like a pretty pink home fit for a baby girl. One of the Bible verses lifted my soul every time I read it. "For you created my inmost being; you knit me together in my mother's womb. I praise you for I am fearfully and wonderfully made; your works are wonderful, I know that full well" (Psalm 139:13-14). How fitting!

Our nurse spent a lot of time with us. Her name was Jen. She was very blunt but provided great care. Many of the NICU nurses looked very young to me. When I first met Jen, I could tell by her work and her confident advice that she was experienced and had spent some years in the NICU. She was definitely Grace's advocate. I called the NICU nurses drill sergeants, but I meant it as a compliment. They ran a tight ship and made sure it stayed that way. I knew it needed to be that way in a critical setting. Jen always double-checked to make sure we washed our hands before we came near Grace. I decided to play some music for Grace, but Jen told me to turn it off. She said Grace was still too sensitive to noise, light, and touch. I started to change Grace's diaper as another younger nurse had shown me the previous day. Jen said in a strong and loud voice, "What are you doing? Who said you could do that?"

It took me off guard as I nervously said, "Uh, uh, uh, another nurse said I could do it."

With a disgusted look on her face she said, "I never allow parents to change diapers on a critical baby who is on an oscillator and has an umbilical line. If that line gets pulled out, she could bleed to death!"

I was not used to being talked to as if I did not know what I was doing, especially as a nurse. But Jen was doing her job and making sure she got the message across. I respected that. I looked back at Jen and said, "No problem! You do not have to worry because I do not want to do it anymore!"

Jen taught us many things on that day and in the days to come. She told us how to get Grace used to our scent. We would sleep with a small burp rag every couple of nights. The rags had Grace's name on them. The nurses would use them to make Grace's bed and would put one near her nose. Grace could smell us even when we were not there.

That next morning on March 24—day four—Josh had to go back to work. He really had a hard time with this. He was afraid he would miss something important. We discussed all of his options concerning work. We knew Grace was going to have a long stay, and Josh had only one week of vacation left. We would need that vacation time for Grace's surgery and for when Grace would come home. He could not take off without vacation time because we needed to keep our medical benefits. So Josh did what he needed to do and went to work that day.

I could not sleep the night before, so I worked on a birth announcement and bugged Grace's night nurse with phone calls. That morning I got up early and headed toward the hospital. I do not know how I woke up with enthusiasm with such lack of sleep. I almost ran through the parking garage and the hallways because I was so excited to see Grace again. By the time I got into the lobby, my cell phone started ringing. First it was our lawyer Kim. She wanted a full report on Grace's condition. She then described all of the ways we could complete the adoption paperwork. After explaining our options in detail, she slowly said, "What do you think?" I reassured her that we were not worried about the paperwork at all. I told her that we trusted her and Mallory to make decisions and that we were not worried about Lizzy changing her mind. I told her that we just needed to focus on the baby. I paced as we talked. As soon as I finished returning some calls that I missed, I did a walking sprint upstairs.

When I reached the NICU, I had to slow down for the daily routine. Sign in at the front desk, put on my name badge, drop off my lunch in the kitchen, scrub in, rush to Grace's bedside, ask the nurse for a report, and hold Grace's hand and head. Then I sat there staring at her most of the time. One of the preemie books I read said that it's good to sing to them, even if you cannot sing well. I sang *Amazing Grace* to her every day, usually in a whisper. Since she always had a nurse at her bedside, I had to swallow my pride and sing despite the fact that I am not a singer. I often tried to sing when the nurse would get supplies so she did not have to listen to me singing off key.

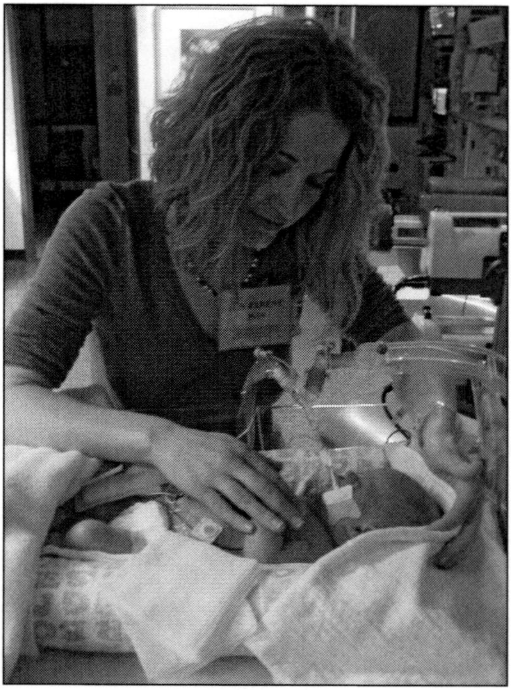

I was able to see the medical team that day. They said they were able to wean Grace to lower settings on the oscillator overnight. They were pleased with this. Her oxygen saturations were still keeping up. The team was worried about her low heart rate. They did a few heart tests: an echocardiogram, EKG, and x-ray of the heart. All of this looked okay. The doctor even came back to say that the x-ray showed a little more of the left lung open. He said he was not sure why and hoped to have her on a regular ventilator within a day. This would allow them to get a CT scan and a surgical consult. A CT would give a better picture than the x-ray. We had been waiting for this next step to find out more of what to expect. We had been told daily by many different medical professionals that the mass removal would be another large hurdle for Grace. They said it would be a major surgery and to expect a "long road" in the hospital. They told us they would have to crack open Grace's sternum to be able to remove the lung to make room for the heart and the other lung. No one would ever give us an estimated time for her length of hospital stay. All we were told was it would be many months.

Grace had been very swollen from pulmonary hypertension and edema. Over the first few days they performed tests on almost all of her organs. The doctor had told us that critical babies often have multi-organ failure. But our little Grace did not. She did become jaundiced and we had to add the UV lamps to all of her other equipment. She had to wear a mask over her eyes to protect them. I really missed seeing her eyes. We were told the jaundice was the least of our worries. She lost some of her swelling and her weight was down to 4 lbs 13 oz. She was still on Versed to keep her calm and still, but she often twitched and jerked as a side effect.

We met some of the other families in our pod and got to know them well. One mother and father across from us had been there with their adorable baby girl for five months. They both came straight to the hospital after work to sit with little Macy every day. The mother, Kate, had hopes of going home in the near future. Kate always had a smile on her face and had encouraging words to share. This was inspiring for me. It gave me confidence that we could get through this too, even if it was a long road. Visiting with others in similar situations seemed to help the time pass easily. A few of us laughed together and cried together. After I told Kate that Grace was adopted, she said, "Well that makes more sense now." The day Grace was born I wore fitted jeans and a fitted shirt. I had put on make-up and fixed my hair because I knew we would be taking pictures. Apparently the mothers had discussed that I didn't look like I had just given birth. They probably all hated me. I got a good chuckle and had some fun with that.

The Miller couple was there with their third child. We saw them often and enjoyed their conversation. They had been in the NICU several years before with one of their other children, so they were able to give us some tips on how to live the NICU life. We also saw some very sick babies all alone, and we saw other things that we did not want to see. I tried to turn my head every time I passed the tiny one-pound baby in the same pod as Grace. I just kept thinking that baby would not make it. He looked so fragile. Another baby that was right next to us never had any family there. He was very ill. I wanted so badly to just go over and talk to him and hold him, but I knew this would not be allowed. The sixty-four bed level 4 NICU was full the entire time we were there. They even had an overflow unit where they had to move some of the children.

I met with our hospital social worker for the first time. I found out that we were not supposed to be having visitors since we were not Grace's legal guardians, and this had been overlooked during the holiday weekend. We were not allowed to bring anyone but ourselves back to see her. She was nice but stern while explaining this. I felt like we had done something bad, and we were being punished for it. Thank goodness it was overlooked for the weekend. Our family would have gone crazy. I am quite sure there would have been beating on the doors and grown women trying to climb up four stories to enter a window. Someone would have gone to jail. My friend Phoebe was already on her way to sit with me when I got this news. I was really looking forward to some adult conversation. Pheobe had to make plans for two babysitters for her three kids, Emma, Claire, and Phillip. How could I tell her to turn around and go home? Two friends from work were coming on their lunch break and more family in the afternoon. My good friend Kristen was planning to come soon. I had it all scheduled to get through the day without Josh. I felt the panic. *What would I do? How could they treat us like this? We were her parents.* I felt like I was being treated like the outsider who broke the rules.

I called Kim right away. I told her what was going on and told her, for the first time, that this was something I would not be able to handle. I could tell she was really listening to what I was saying, and she agreed to do her best to help with the situation. It may seem small to have no visitors, but for me on that day it was my breaking point. I needed visitors to help me cope. Josh would not be able to be with me every day. How could I sit in the quiet room having only the hum of the machines and the beeping of the monitors to listen to? No TV, no radio, no food, and no sleeping allowed. I just knew I would lose my mind. I needed my friends and family to keep me strong! I explained all of this to the social worker. I told her about all of my visitors planning to come that day. She seemed to soften a little and told me that my friend who was almost there could come in, but I would have to call and cancel everyone else. She told me she knew it must be hard and that she was sorry. But there would be no more exceptions to the rules. We had to have notarized permission from Lizzy to bring in visitors. I figured this paperwork would take days. I knew Lizzy would approve. This was so frustrating.

Within a few hours the hospital social worker came by and told me that my lawyer Kim had taken care of things. "What do you mean? I can have visitors?" I said.

She told me that Lizzy signed a power of attorney. Kim gets stuff done! Within that short time she had the papers typed, signed by Lizzy in the hospital, notarized, and faxed to our social worker. I wanted to give her a big high five, bear hug, or something to show my gratitude. I was so impressed. What an ingenious idea. Now we could make medical decisions even though the adoption was not final. Lizzy was happy with this too. Lizzy told Kim she was mad that the hospital was giving us trouble. Lizzy wanted us making the decisions. It worked out for everyone, even for most of the visitors. I still had to turn some people away that day. I felt badly that a few people drove all the way to the city to see us, and I could not let them see Grace. But the restriction was not there for long.

We worked on a few other legal issues that day. Grace was born in one state but was transferred to another. There were different ways that the paperwork could be approached, and Kim explained all of them. I heard a lot of blah, blah, blah again; I tried to understand. We put our trust in our lawyer and let her do her job. Kim exceeded our expectations in everything she did.

That same afternoon the critical care transport team brought a new baby to our pod. I watched the four as they worked gently and diligently with this little life. It was the same team that brought Grace. I waved at the main guy, Chris, who explained everything so gently and thoroughly the day Grace was born. When things were settled, I walked over to say hello. I thanked Chris for all he had done for Grace. I told him if he had a chance he should come to visit her. I almost did not say anything to him. I knew how busy and intense his job was. He smiled and took off his gloves. He went into a brisk walk and headed a few beds down toward Grace. He was excited to see her. I was glad that I had said something. He stopped at Grace's side. He looked her up and down with a smile on his face. He went on and on about how good it was that she was weaning off of the oscillator. He was a highly trained and experienced respiratory therapist. He looked at all of her settings and said that he was very pleased.

Chris and I discussed his job. I asked him what his longest transport was. He said in a slow southern drawl, "Do you mean by jet or vehicle?"

My eyes widened. "Are you kidding me?"

Chris explained how teams transport children to and from other countries and travel all over the United States. Then he added, "You know you are in one of the best hospitals in the world, right?"

I know that Chris was another one of the human angels God had sent to us. He made me realize how thankful I should be that we lived close enough to the hospital to make daily visits.

Chris told me how nice Josh was and asked how he was doing. He told me how uplifting it was to see a family with smiles and hope. He said it seems that the worst things happen to the nicest people. I took this as a compliment, and it brightened my day. He was so kind and sincere. I asked if I could take his picture. This was someone I did not want to forget because he took the time to do more than his job required. He cared. He cared enough to stop and check in. He cared enough to smile. He cared enough to ask if he could come back and check on us again. Phoebe was still there visiting with me and took our picture. Once again I was in trouble with Jen, our drill sergeant nurse, who was helping admit a new baby. She yelled, "What are you doing? You cannot take pictures of other patients!"

She was so intimidating. I could barely get the words out quickly enough as she charged toward us with her nostrils flaring. "Uh, uh, the baby is not in the pi-pi-pi-picture! We are taking it of Chris," I said. She just turned around and went back to work. Even though our nurse almost pounced on me, I was really glad I had that picture.

I walked back to Grace. Jen was taking care of her. I was not sure if she was in soldier mode or nurse mode. I was worried I was still in trouble with her. I made small talk and she seemed okay. I told her how awestruck I was at what the transport team does. She told me that she has taken care of babies from all over the country. She said there are not many parents around even though it is a giant NICU. She said many of the parents live hours and states away. They have other kids and have to go back to work. It is difficult to visit when they live so far away. I felt so thankful that day! How do these parents do it? How can they go on with life and work when their baby is miles away in the NICU? That daily forty-minute drive back and forth suddenly seemed like nothing at all.

The day only seemed to get better if that was possible. I found out that Lizzy was doing well and had been released from the hospital. Her neighbor was taking care of her. I was relieved that she had someone to help her. I left the hospital and picked up Evan. He and Mom had made two dozen sugar cookies. Sugar cookies were something I could eat and eat, even when nothing else sounded good. I sat on my mother's red bar stool by the kitchen island with flour and icing all over it. I ate cookie after cookie. They were soft and the icing was sweet. They just went along with the day. While I stuffed my mouth, I told Mom, Dad, and Evan all of the good events of the day. Then I went home and played Hi-ho Cheerio with Evan. I could not wait for Josh to get home from work so I could tell him all of the stories from the day. We were looking forward to the next day. Josh was off every Tuesday, and he would get to go to the hospital with me. We had high hopes of Grace moving to a normal ventilator and of us meeting with the surgical team. It would be a relief to hear a little bit of a plan even if it meant a long road. All things considered, this seemed to be a good day, the kind of day that you are pretty sure the next day could not compete with. We praised and thanked God that we could have such a day. We never imagined what would come next.

CHAPTER THIRTEEN

Tuesday

On Tuesday morning, March 25, 2008—day five—Josh and I dropped Evan off at school and headed for the hospital. We were anxious to see if Grace could be moved to a regular ventilator. We could not wait to get that CT scan to help us prepare some kind of plan. Having a plan helps me function. If I know what to expect I can deal with things better. It's the unknown that drives me crazy. We knew we would probably have to wait most of the day for the test results. We also knew there was a chance that it would not get done, and we would have to wait longer.

That's just how things go in the hospital most of the time. We discussed the possible events of the day in the car. We talked to each other about being hopeful, but not letting ourselves be disappointed. We arrived at the hospital around 10:00 a.m. We went through the daily routine—look all over for a good parking spot, hand over our driver's license, sign in, put on our badges, sign in again at the NICU, drop off our lunch in the kitchen, scrub in, and head toward Grace.

When we finally arrived at Grace's bed, we noticed that the oscillator had been replaced by a conventional ventilator. We could not believe they had done it already. I was breathing fast. We had so many questions. The nurse was not there. I noticed the ventilator was on its lowest setting. We were dumfounded. How could this be? We both were almost in tears. Then the medical team saw us and came walking toward us. Dr. Johnson told us that the CT scan was done. We did not expect that! I started breathing faster. I knew we were getting ready to hear some kind of plan. We were getting ready to hear about our baby's future. I could not believe they had done so much so early. I wanted to know what they had learned from the CT scan, yet I didn't. It seemed like we had waited so long for this test. Dr. Johnson had a smile on his face and was wearing one of his wild shirts with the large seventies collar and colorful floral print. The other members of the team stood around looking at him. Then he said, "The scan showed the lung open and no mass. The lung still looks a little foggy, but it is all the way open."

Josh and I looked at each other in disbelief and shock. I said, "What does this mean?" probably a total of five times with a barely audible, shaky voice. *How can a mass open up? That is not possible*. I began to feel light-headed. I locked my arm into Josh's.

The doctor explained, "First of all it means no surgery because there is nothing to remove." Josh's eyes were gigantic, and he kept hitting my upper arm with the back of his hand like it was some kind of reflex. He did not say a word. I wanted to grab his hand and put it down, but my brain was not able to function at the level to tell my hand what to do. I think he could not speak and wanted me to ask the questions. As we smiled, tears began to roll down our cheeks—tears were rare for Josh. I kept asking, "No surgery—how could this be? Everyone said she would need major surgery!"

The doctor replied, "It's a real medical mystery."

The doctor described some other possibilities. It could be Respiratory Distress Syndrome (RDS) or a severe infection. But he said that her symptoms did not fit well with those explanations. We told him we knew it was a miracle because of all the prayers. We did not need an explanation. He told us that he wanted to discuss his thoughts with the radiologist and some other doctors. He said he would come back to talk with us later that day.

We waited to tell anyone. We wanted to see what the other doctors had to say. It just seemed way too good to be true. Dr. Johnson came back within the hour. He said that the doctors were going to take away the CCAM diagnosis, and there was no other diagnosis for her lungs at that time. He seemed to be bothered by the fact that he could not explain what was going on, probably because he was a doctor in one of the best hospitals in the world and was used to having explanations. We just kept telling him that we did not need an explanation.

He began to explain what we could expect. He said that Grace would be completely off the ventilator by the next day. He explained that they were able to put Grace on a low setting for the conventional ventilator because there was a small air leak around her endotracheal tube. At that time, Grace was keeping her oxygen levels up on her own. So they knew she could breathe on her own without much help.

The next thing they did was pull her arterial line. Then they started weaning her off the morphine and Versed. They decided to give feedings through her nasogastric tube by the next day also. They said that basically all we had to do to get her home was to teach her to eat and make sure she was having bowel movements and weight gain. Every lab test was looking good. This was all in one day. In five days we went from planning a possible funeral, to needing a major surgery and Grace being in the hospital for months, to just needing to teach her how to eat. We were told that we could likely take her home around her due date, as is typical for all preemies. This was just seven weeks away. We were amazed!

We walked down to the hospital lobby. We told almost everyone we saw about the events—no joke. We sat down and called Lizzy first. She paused, sniffled, and said, "Thank you, God!" several times. She was so excited. She said that she knew all along Grace would be okay. Her faith was strong. Josh wanted to send a Bible verse in a text message to everyone else. We did not have our Bible with us, but we had a devotional book in our bag. We chose Psalm 107:20: "He sent forth his word and healed them; he rescued them from the grave."

We sent the Bible verse first and then sent the news because they both would not fit in one text. The calls and text messages starting pouring in from friends and family. They wanted every detail. No one understood what was happening, and we caused some confusion. Some thought Grace was dying, some thought she was healed, and some thought we sent out a verse of hope. It was not our intent to confuse everyone—we knew what we meant. But we had some explaining to do to everyone else.

As the text messages were still making our phones jingle like crazy, I unexpectedly saw Danny. Danny was a drug rep that I saw occasionally at events and work functions over the last eight years because our jobs were related to dialysis. Danny reminds me of a social, fluffy teddy bear. The ironic part about seeing Danny on that Tuesday was that Danny and I were at the same conference when I received the call about our first child Evan. He was the first one to know we were parents and the first one to give me a giant hug. Then he made sure everyone at work heard the news as well.

So when I saw Danny on Grace's miracle day walking through the small lobby on the main floor of

Children's Health Hospital, I was in awe. I had not seen him for months. Now he was the first person we saw face to face that we could tell about Grace's big news. Once again, he was excited for us and bounced around as we told him the story. I appreciated his enthusiasm. There was something very huggable about Danny. He hugged us both and got the word going through the grapevine again for me. The odds of him walking through the lobby right when we were there had to be less than the chance of being struck by lightning. Maybe God knew I needed the person who could give the best hugs. I knew there had to be a very special reason. Danny was yet another one of our human angels.

I thought on that miracle day that I would burst like a marshmallow in the microwave if things got any better. One of our concerns had been that the nurses could not hear bowel sounds. Grace was still getting all of her nutrition through her veins. It could be dangerous if her bowels became "lazy" from not being used. We were told that the bowel sounds would increase when they started oral feedings. By that afternoon her two nurses were excited because they heard good bowel sounds; Grace had not even started oral feedings yet!

Many of the nurses and staff heard the news of the miracle. The word traveled fast through the large NICU that day. Many staff came by to meet Grace and to congratulate us. Kate came over to find out what was going on. She had tears rolling down her cheeks as she hugged us. She told me that the first day she saw Grace she wondered if Grace was going to make it. I am sure this had to be bittersweet news for Kate. I know she longed for Macy to get some good news. Yet I know she was happy for us. Grace caused a lot of commotion on that floor that day.

We wanted to tell the world! We did not want to leave Grace, but we wanted to embrace Evan and our whole family. It was definitely a time for celebration. We picked up our favorite carry-out Mexican dinner, sent out a text that we would be home, and our whole family showed up to celebrate with us. There were around fifteen people in our home and many more than fifteen tears of joy. Josh said the most beautiful and praising prayer. We all enjoyed being together. We laughed, played, and ate. Our two nieces and two nephews danced with Evan to upbeat music. That day I had a feeling of floating on a cloud. There was no worry, no physical pain, and no stress. I even enjoyed doing the laundry and washing all of Grace's clothes to take back to the hospital. Joy flooded over every other feeling. I felt so alive and happy. It felt as if nothing could ever take that feeling away, like I would never feel sadness or worries again. I imagined that was a slight glimpse of what heaven must feel like.

Lizzy called and left a message that she had shared the story with many people in her life. Some of the people were people who were unsure of their faith. There were so many touched by Grace's miracle on that day. I could not wait to see what the next day had in store. I knew this feeling would not last forever and that bad things would happen again. That is just how life is.

I really cannot explain in words how I felt that day. Many others said that same thing. All I know is that God the Father gave us an amazing gift on Tuesday, March 25, 2008. On a typical Tuesday to most of the world, we received Tuesday's grace. God's abounding grace poured out and filled our tiny baby girl. She was alive and well. God gave us the gift of hope. "'For I know the plans I have for you,' declares the Lord, 'plans to prosper you and not to harm you, plans to give you hope and a future'" (Jeremiah 29:11). We were in the middle of a modern day miracle!

CHAPTER FOURTEEN

Life Moving Forward

The day after the miracle we were able to take Grace completely off of the ventilator and place her on oxygen by nasal cannula (a tube next to her nose). Her blood count was normal for the first time. Her x-ray was still showing her lung completely open, and her heart was now in the correct place. Dr. Johnson said the left lung was still a little foggy, so the team planned to monitor her lungs daily with x-rays. They also put a nasogastric tube down her nose and into her stomach so that she could start getting small amounts of nutrition into her stomach to start preparing her gastrointestinal tract to work. I worked with Grace using the pacifier most of that day. The nurses wanted her to use it to learn how to suck in order to prepare her for bottle feedings. They stopped her morphine and Versed. She became more active and no longer appeared so lifeless. She had her first bowel movement that day. That was good news too! We were told that she may not be able to make sounds or cry for a while because her vocal cords were most likely irritated from the ventilator tubes. They were wrong again. That day, Grace cried. She cried a gentle, sweet, quiet sound, a sound that I was so happy to hear.

They put a new peripheral IV line in her scalp. With this new access they would be able to pull out her umbilical line. We had been told that we could hold Grace when she was off the ventilator and her umbilical line was pulled. She had two more bowel movements, and we were told this would help to improve her jaundice. The team was busy with our daughter that day, and it was all good. What we were most excited about was holding our new, precious baby girl in our arms for the first time—we waited and waited and waited. We had a different nurse and a trainee that day. We were really missing Jen. The new nurse was not used to us, and we were not used to her. We kept asking when we would get to hold Grace. We kept waiting. Finally, after four in the afternoon, the nurse told us it was time.

I got to hold Grace first. The nurse had me sit in a chair right next to Grace's bed with a pillow on my lap. She started moving lines and IV poles around. She then swaddled her in a blanket. She gently lifted her and moved her just a couple of feet into my open arms. Grace felt like a bundle of feathers. She was so tiny. She was warm, wrapped in my arms and next to my chest. It felt so marvelous. I placed my lips on her head and took in a deep, sweet breath. I sat and stared for a while. The nurse kept asking if we were okay and watched the monitors. Grace seemed perfectly comfortable. I think the feel of a human embrace was something new, yet wonderful to her. I was finally holding our baby girl for the first time! While I held her, I just knew I would get to hold her for years to come. Josh was ready for his turn. It took all three of us to safely make the transfer to Josh without pulling on any lines. I enjoyed watching them together as much as I enjoyed holding her. Josh looked like a giant next to her tiny body.

I did not like looking at the IV line in her head, so I placed that side against the pillow. I knew she had to have it, but something about the line being in her head really bothered me. One nurse told me that the head is the least painful place for babies to have a line; that helped a little.

Now that we could hold Grace in our arms, it somehow made everything feel a little more real. The nurse soon told us we had a visitor. A long time pastor friend of the family, Randy, came by that day to pray with us. We all walked out into the waiting room and sat down. We were able to share our story of Grace's miracle with him. I know he has heard many miraculous stories during his many years of being a pastor. I am sure he has heard many sad stories. But as we shared our story of Grace, we once again saw tears of joy.

The next day I was looking forward to time at home with my little guy. I had missed him so much, and I knew that he needed some mommy time. He had been going through so much too. He was glad to be home with me. We were ready to kick back and relax together. But I had received a number of phone calls throughout that day, so my focus ended up on the phone calls.

We did have some drama that day. No one could reach Lizzy. Her social worker and both lawyers were trying to reach her. They left messages and she was not returning phone calls. She was supposed to meet with her lawyer to sign the papers the next day. Our lawyer, Kim, and our social worker, Mallory, were worried about what might be going on. Kim was trying to figure out the best way to do the paperwork. She and I went over many details related to custody and insurance coverage.

I told everyone I would try to reach Lizzy to see what was going on. When I called Lizzy, she answered. We talked for a long time. She said that she was not changing her mind about the adoption, but that she was worried about the changes that signing the papers might bring. Lizzy was afraid she might not get to hold or see Grace again. I reassured her that she would see and hold baby Grace. After that conversation, I talked with Mallory. She told me that in her twenty-two years of work, Lizzy was the first birthmother who had a baby so critical that she did not get to hold the baby before the papers were signed. Lizzy's fears made sense to me. She needed to hold in her arms the baby she carried in her womb for seven months. I notified everyone after I talked with her. I had to convince Kim I was not worried about the papers getting signed. Josh was not worried either. Josh and I still had faith as tall and wide as a mountain from witnessing our miracle. We knew that God would not change everything now.

Despite my hours on the phone, Evan was happy playing in his room with his Legos and trucks. I think he was just relieved to be home. I later dropped Evan off at Phoebe's house for the evening as I headed for the hospital. Phoebe handed me a sack lunch. She knew eating had not been a top priority for me, and she knew exactly what I needed. Her homemade chicken salad sandwich tasted so good! It was much better than fast food and much cheaper! She was also taking her three kids for haircuts that day, and since I had already missed two of Evan's haircut appointments, she offered to take him too. So the poor, shaggy-haired kid got a haircut! There were many people like Phoebe who did little things for us that might seem insignificant, but these things added up to help us keep our sanity. I am not sure how we would have made it through without all of the help.

While I was driving and eating my food, my phone rang. I still had some miles to drive, so I talked in detail with a close friend who is an MD and a medical genius in her field. I really consider her more of a mother figure because she is older than I am, and she has given great advice during some of the difficult times in my life. She wanted to know every detail. It was the first time that I talked about the medical aspects of our miracle to someone. She just kept saying over and over, "I cannot believe it!" She laughed a joyful laugh. We do not have the same beliefs about God, and we have always been very open about that. She told me that Grace's whole story made her question her spirituality. That made me grin from ear to ear.

As soon as we finished our conversation, I arrived at the hospital running again. I knew I would be able to hold my baby in my arms all day. I could hold her close and tell her that I was there and would never leave her. Once I arrived, I told her the worst was over. Her little body was no longer limp. She was allowed to feel a human embrace. Her eyes were alive, and she gazed into my eyes many times. There were no visitors that day. It was just me and Grace. I sang "Amazing Grace" as always. Then I sang "Twinkle,

Twinkle Little Star," "Jesus Loves Me," and "This Little Light of Mine," and I even made up a new song called "Princess Grace." I am sure other parents made up songs too since we sat all day with no TV, radio, or adults to talk with. I used some of the time to write Jen, our favorite nurse, a note about the events we were expecting the next day. I spoke with the charge nurse and requested Jen to be Grace's nurse.

There were a lot of important events on Friday, March 28—day eight. Mallory and Kim arrived at the hospital to sign papers. Lizzy came with Mallory. I could not wait for all of them to see Grace. I wrote in Jen's note that Friday would be very special. I wanted her to know that Lizzy had not yet held Grace. I warned her that Lizzy might have a lot of questions about the medical equipment. I was afraid that Lizzy might be frightened by it.

Lizzy went in and spent forty-five minutes alone with Grace. I was not sure how Lizzy would react to the visit. Jen had put a small red bow on Grace's head. She remade her bed and placed all of Grace's stuffed animals and gifts around her. She did a great job welcoming Lizzy. As Lizzy walked out of the NICU into the waiting room, she had a smile on her face and no tears. She told us that there must have been many people praying because, even though she was so glad to hold Grace, she felt at peace leaving her.

Lizzy left the hospital that day and went straight over to sign the legal papers to give Josh and me legal custody. The law required another month of social worker visits before we could make the adoption final. A few hours after Lizzy signed the papers, we met with Kim and her assistant in the hospital lobby. We looked for any open space. I sat down at a child-sized table in a child-sized chair. Josh sat on an adult bench on the other side of the table beside Kim and her assistant, and we proceeded to sign. We signed our mountain of papers. I actually signed my name more times than when I bought a house. I did not even care what the papers said. I fully trusted Kim, and I just wanted to get back to our baby girl, so I signed as fast as I could. *What was the worse thing I could be signing? To give my house away? My car? Who cares! I am a Mom with a wonderful son and a new baby girl!*

We wanted to celebrate our legal custody. Later that day we met Lizzy and Mallory for lunch. It was nice to get out of the hospital for a little while. We talked and visited with no "business" to take care of. We did not have to discuss plans. Everyone seemed to be at ease. We just talked about life.

We returned to Grace that afternoon and offered our baby her first bottle—what an experience! She spit most of it out. The amount in the bottle was tiny, only about two tablespoons. We had to hold her a certain way to keep her from choking. We had to constantly squeeze her cheeks and lift her chin to stimulate the sucking reflex. We had to learn her cues for when she needed to breathe. Grace did not know how to suck, swallow, and breathe at the same time. The first few times we tried to feed her, I thought she might never learn how to eat. But the nurses assured us that she would eventually learn. Jen (a.k.a. drill sergeant) told us we would never get her home until we got her to eat. She said, "Do you want to take that baby home?" We of course said "Yes." Then she said, "Then you had better wake that baby up and get her to eat!" I wanted to salute and say, "Yes Ma'am!"

My parents, Grace's Maw Maw and Paw Paw, came to visit, and had bought more preemie clothes. They were so cute, but still too big. Grace actually got to wear her first outfit the very next day. The jaundice was better, so the lamps were gone and Grace could now wear clothes. Jen put another bow in her hair. Her outfit had big flowers covering her hands. It said *pretty girl* on the front. All of the nurses were commenting on how cute she looked. Jen taught us a lot that day. She said she wanted to start preparing us for home. That phrase sounded wonderful!

CHAPTER FIFTEEN

A Few More Ups and Downs

Just days after floating on a cloud, a couple of conversations started to bring me down. I asked a nurse practitioner for some of Grace's medical records. This seemed to make her nervous. My intentions were to learn the medical facts for myself and to share them with others. I wanted us to have the records to look at years down the road so I could remember what a miracle this was. I had no malicious intent. I also knew that I had a right to those records. Her nervousness made me suspicious.

The nurse practitioner agreed to show me the first and last x-rays. There was a definite difference. Even though I am not an x-ray expert, the improvements were obvious to me. She explained the first one as showing a white-out area over the whole left lung with an hourglass appearance. She said this appearance is typical of RDS (respiratory distress syndrome) where the alveoli (the small functioning unit of the lung where oxygen exchange occurs) do not function from lack of surfactant. She explained how this would be an issue that would not show up until after birth. She also explained how it is not typical for only one lung to produce surfactant and not the other. So this explanation would not fit well with Grace since she had one bad lung and one good lung. She seemed to get more frustrated and nervous as I asked more questions. I tried to reassure her that I was not questioning her knowledge, but I wanted to understand what she was saying. When I asked her what the three neonatologists saw prior to birth, she explained that doctors often make mistakes with sonograms. I told her I saw the sonogram pictures that showed the heart pushed over and the abnormal lung. I asked her why there was such a huge amount of amniotic fluid that caused premature labor. She replied again that sonograms are not always accurate. She also said that it is sometimes normal for healthy hearts to shift more to one side. I thought to myself, *How could ten or more sonograms and three specialists all be wrong? And, why did the heart end up shifting back if it was 'normally' shifted?*

The nurse practitioner tried to sound firm and confident in what she was saying, but nothing fit together for me. She seemed to be talking in circles, and her voice was defensive. I do not understand why some people cannot just say, "I honestly cannot explain it," like Dr. Johnson did. I felt more confident in him for just being honest. I know how complicated our bodies and science are. We cannot expect doctors to be able to explain everything. I went away from this conversation feeling frustrated. I felt unsure of her intent. Did she want to convince me that this was not a miracle? It sure seemed that way. It was as if she were trying her hardest to let medical diagnosis and misdiagnosis explain it. Did I make her nervous because I asked so many questions and wanted medical records? Did I make her nervous because I was an RN? I don't know. Near the end of the conversation, I explained to her that Grace was a miracle because of many prayers and our God answering those prayers. I told her she did not have to keep trying to explain. She had no comment.

This conversation caused me to be discouraged and frustrated. One other nurse whom I respected caused similar discouragement. When I told her about our belief in miracles and what the doctor said about this being a "medical mystery," she said that the doctor had to say that because he would not say that another doctor made a misdiagnosis. I realized she said this without reading all of the medical history. I also told myself that she was not there when the doctor kept coming back to tell us he was trying to find an answer. I later received all of the medical records and read the x-ray radiology reports from Children's Health Hospital that still gave Grace the CCAM diagnosis even after birth.

Why are people so afraid to accept a miracle? Even if they do not believe it, why would they not want others to believe in it? A Bible verse came to my mind. "Turn away from godless chatter and the opposing ideas of what is falsely called knowledge, which some have professed and in so doing have wandered from the faith. Grace be with you" (1 Timothy 6:20-21). I had to use this verse because it fit so well, but also because I found the "Grace be with you" ironically funny!

I have heard many preachers speak on the topic of doubt. If Satan and his evil can cause doubt, it can lead to questioning of faith. There is a war of good and evil on this earth. Planting doubts is the devil's tool. Satan will use anything or anyone he can to keep the spotlight off of God. I have heard pastors say that any time you set out to do something good, you will run into trials. God never promised us this life would be easy. Jesus said, "I have told you these things, so that in me you may have peace. In this world you will have trouble. But take heart! I have overcome the world" (John 16:33).

I had been high on answered prayers. I wanted to tell the world. Then, two short conversations planted doubts. This was just the first of many trials in trying to tell our story. *Was this really a miracle after all? Was it just misdiagnosis?* I was so confident before. I knew there was some spiritual warfare going on here. Satan would never want me telling everyone how God answers prayers and still performs miracles. Well, too bad Satan! I turned to God in prayer, thought about how the conversations did not make any sense, and got over those doubts. So on with the story!

With every new day there was change and more exciting events to add to Grace's story. Over the next couple of weeks Grace improved daily. Josh and I had computer access in the lounge at the hospital and spent some time building a March of Dimes website for "Team Grace." It kept us occupied and made us feel like we could do something to help other babies and parents in our situation. A March of Dimes walk was coming to the city, and we wanted to be at the front of the line. We were so thankful for the hospital and staff, yet we often felt helpless. It felt good to be able to give something back and raise money for other babies and families. Josh and I occasionally tried to step out of the NICU to do other positive things. We had a date one night at the hospital and explored the many hallways. We went to the library to work more on March of Dimes, and we ate in the cafeteria for the first time. We spent some time in the Ronald McDonald house testing their food and couches. They even had television! Having a fun date in a hospital may be hard to understand, but it is all perspective. It really raised our morale and helped us focus on the positive.

Over the next several days Grace was regulating her own temperature and was able to advance out of the warmer. Then she was put into a big girl's crib. It was a normal crib, just smaller in size. She was weaned off of the oxygen to breathe the air in the room. At first she received most of her feedings through her nasogastric tube. As she learned to use a bottle, they increased the amount and number of bottles daily. She still drooled most of her bottle, even though it was only four teaspoons of formula. We still had to squeeze her cheeks, lift her chin, and put her on her side so she would not choke and stop breathing. The alarm often showed low oxygen levels during her feedings. We had to watch her cues and pull the bottle out when she needed a breath.

We became more confident with time and were more and more involved in Grace's care. It became harder to leave her. When we were not there, we called and checked on her often. I would wake up in the middle of the night and call. Britney, a night nurse, learned my voice. I had met Britney a few times when we were at the hospital late at night. She was young, thin, and tall, with straight blonde hair. She had a soft, high-pitched voice. She told us she loved taking care of Grace, and I loved knowing that she was there loving on her. She gave her baths in the middle of the night. One night the phone rang at 11:30 p.m. We could see on the caller ID that it was Children's Health Hospital. They had never called us in the twelve days that we had been there. I knew it was too late for paperwork or an insurance call. I felt like I was going to vomit. It had not been long since we had left, and everything had been just fine. It seemed like years before Britney got out what she was trying to say. She said, "I am so sorry but…" My heart sank and all the blood rushed out of my head before she finished. In that moment my mind went over all of the things that could be wrong that would require a late phone call. I remembered our first doctor's words when he told us that preemies can turn bad quickly. *Was she sick? Was she going to die after having a miracle? Wouldn't it take something big for this type of a phone call?* Britney then finished, "We are going to move Grace to another unit." Whew! What a relief! I could take a breath again.

She told us they had five admissions that night and had to move five of the most stable babies to the overflow unit next door. Hearing that Grace was deemed one of the five most stable was calming. Britney said that she did not want us to walk into the unit in the morning and panic because Grace was not there. She did the right thing by calling us. I would have attacked the nurses with questions trying to find Grace if I walked in and saw another baby in her space. That would have produced horrible thoughts for sure!

I was not happy about the move at first. I was used to most of her nurses, and they knew how to take good care of Grace. They were used to us, and we knew what to expect from each other. Britney told me she was really sad and did not want Grace to be moved. I was worried for Grace leaving the sounds, smells, and voices that she had gotten used to over the past twelve days. This was a shock because they had told us we would be in the NICU until Grace was discharged. I had no idea what to expect in the overflow unit. Just as we were getting into a routine, things had to change.

When I arrived the next morning, I changed my mind. It was so much better! Our room had a bathroom, a fridge, a T.V., a window, a closet, tons of room, and even a small bed if I wanted to stay. It seemed like hospital life in the lap of luxury. I looked up and told God I was sorry that I had doubted him again. I was allowed to eat and drink in the room. I had my own sink to scrub in. I did not have to anxiously wait in line to scrub before I could see our baby. I could have more than two visitors at a time, and children were allowed in this unit. I was so excited that Evan would finally get to meet his little sister. And Andrew, Kenzy, Payton, and Ava would finally get to meet their cousin. After I looked over Grace's new temporary home, Kristen, the nurse practitioner, came in to visit.

Kristen told me that Grace's labs were good, her x-rays were good, and there were no other concerns. She said that all we had to do to go home was to have Grace eating, having stools, and gaining some weight. I asked if we could take her home and do the NG feedings at home. Kristen quickly said, "No, because we are getting close to her not needing them." Grace was taking two bottles per day. They told us that most babies were able to go home around their actual due date and to still expect that. That meant we would have several more weeks in the hospital. I sent Lizzy all of the updates by text message.

Lizzy was able to visit. We talked about John, the birthfather, signing the legal custody papers. John had told Lizzy he knew they could not take care of Grace, and he was ready to place her in our care. We knew Kim was traveling that day to meet John and have him sign the papers. Kim told us that John was okay with everything during her visit with him. Even though we had been told John had no problem signing the papers, it was still a relief when it actually happened.

I did not have much time to think about the events with John. Grace was beginning to keep me more active—she had her first fit. She started crying during her NG feeding. I knew something was wrong. Then she had a big bowel movement. While I was cleaning her, she spit up all over. I threw the bed covers off to get them out of the way. Then her EKG sticker came off. She was pulling at her NG tube and scratching her face. I put my hand over the NG tube, and then her oxygen monitor came off her foot. All of her alarms were sounding, she was crying, and there was stool on her lines! I really needed the nurse, and she was nowhere in sight. Usually there were nurses everywhere. Another baby must have been having problems too. I soon figured out that Grace's bottom was raw. I think changing her diaper really hurt, and that was what caused her reaction. Poor baby—she experienced her first diaper rash. I cleaned her up and put on diaper ointment. The nurse finally came to put her monitors back on just as I was getting things under control. I wanted to keep Grace from doing this again. I did not want her to scratch her face. Preemie-sized mittens fell off Grace's hands, so I put on an outfit that covered her hands. I wrapped her up like a burrito, and she was soon fast asleep. She looked like a little angel. That fit wore us both out.

After that episode I did not have any problems finding a nurse. I found out that the medical team was considering a discharge in a few days. I was in shock once again. Everything she did kept amazing me! One of the NP's told me that the "bottle fairy" would come along and bop Grace on the head. I told her that I thought she had done it on that day. Grace started rooting and making little grunts and piggy noises when it was time to eat. I was amazed at how she suddenly took to the bottle and how little she was spitting out. I could not believe that they were going to let us go home one-and-a-half weeks earlier than the earliest expected date. They also took out her IV line from her head that day. I was very pleased about that. She no longer looked like she had an alien antenna. I was looking forward to telling Evan about it face to face.

A child-life specialist came to talk with us about Evan meeting Grace. I was nervous about what Evan would think or do. The specialist brought in some paint, a book, and a video game. She told me Evan might ignore Grace at first, but that was normal.

I was so excited for Evan to finally meet his sister. That evening Josh brought him to the Hospital; I met Josh and Evan in the lobby. Evan was clingy and wanted to be held. We walked the hallways back toward Grace's room. I was so happy to have my whole family together. We walked slowly into the room. Evan was hesitant and quiet. He pointed to the crib. I said, "There is your baby sister."

"Cool!" he said. "Oh, look at that tube in her nose."

We told him that it did not hurt, that it was just for her food. Then he went straight over to paint and play video games. The child specialist was right. We went to the cafeteria to eat, and he danced to the juke box music. Then we went by the playroom at the end of the hallway. When we came back to the room, it was time for Grace's next bottle. Evan wanted to help so we let him. When she whined, he said in a tender voice, "It's okay, baby Grace." He rubbed her head and held her hand. He pushed her nose like a button. He was so sweet and gentle. When we put Grace back in the crib, Evan pulled a chair close and wanted to watch everything she did. He held her hand some more. He pushed back both of her mitten sleeves because he wanted to see and hold her hands. It was late when we finally left to go home. By that time Evan seemed at ease with his baby sister. I was relieved. Seeing our whole family together was magical.

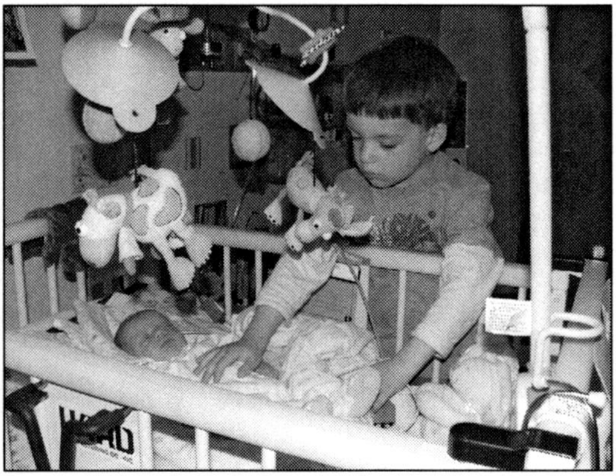

On Saturday, April 6—day seventeen—we had many visitors. Our sisters' families came first. It was time for the cousins to meet Grace for the first time. They all adored Grace and played in the hospital room. They rode in the wagon and played with the nurses. They touched Grace's hands and loved on her. It was a lot of fun. Jann, my mother-in-law, also known as Minny, was happy to stay in the room with Grace while the rest of us went to the cafeteria. Jann got to change her first poopy diaper. She was also there alone when Grace had another fit and pulled out her NG tube! Things did not go as hoped for Minny during this short time, and she was glad to see us arrive back in the room.

Grace was always scratching at her face; she did not like that tube. She was done with it. She had been taking her bottles well, so the nurse agreed to not put the tube back in unless it was needed. We had to do a lot of tickling and waking her up through her feedings, but we got those bottles down and kept that tube out.

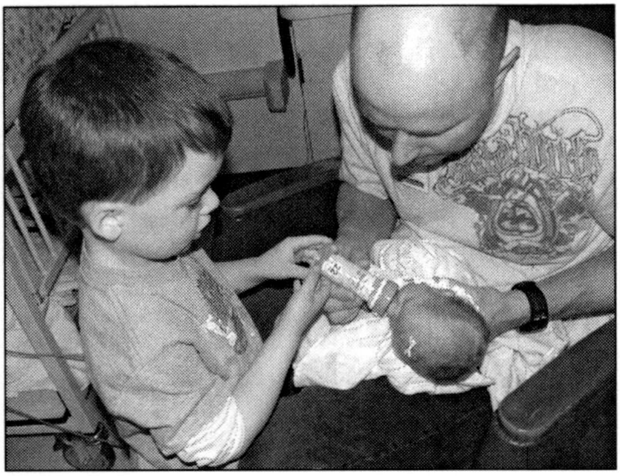

Journal entry April 6, 2008: *We went home late. Grace was comfy and asleep before we left. In the car we were talking about our concerns with our finances and me not working. We reminded ourselves that every time we worry, money comes out of nowhere.*

It was dark and late, but we decided to stop at the end of the driveway to get the mail. I looked through—bills, bills, bills, junk mail, junk mail. Then I noticed a personal envelope and opened it. A check for $100 was tucked inside a thoughtful card. Right then I had a tearful laugh at the irony of our recent conversation and looked up to God with a smile.

On Sunday the medical team came in to talk with us. We met a doctor whom we had not seen before, but he was with a nurse practitioner whom we knew. They told us that Grace had a spell of bradycardia (low heart rate) and low O2 saturation (blood oxygen level). They told us the nurse had to stimulate her to get them back up. I hated that we were not there during that event and decided I would stay every night after that. The doctor said that it could be from her reflux causing vagal nerve stimulation and that they would continue to monitor it closely. The vagus nerve is connected to the heart and digestive tract, so the heart can possibly be irritated by acid reflux. He asked some questions about Grace and our situation. The doctor looked at our pictures hanging above Grace's bed and began to ask about Evan. He asked if he was adopted also. He asked about his health. I told him about the Kawasaki's disease that Evan had at age ten months. He was quite interested, so I told him the details. He said we had been through quite a lot and told us how lucky our kids were to have us. I told him that we were the lucky ones.

Kristen, the NP, stayed to talk with us. She was always kind and interested in Grace. We talked about our kids some more. I found out that she had adopted a baby boy from the hospital. She had been caring for him in the NICU. He was now a teenager. We talked about adoption. She said that it had crossed her mind to adopt again, but she was not sure that she would be able to at her age. I get enthusiastic talking to people who are interested in adoption. I told her I didn't think she was too old and that adoption rules have changed a lot over the years. She seemed to be interested, so I gave her our agency's information. I wondered if God had crossed our paths for a specific reason.

Later that day Lizzy and some of her friends came to the hospital for a visit. They all held Grace. The little girls brought her adorable gifts and sentimental scrapbooks. It was loud in the room at times with a lot of commotion. Grace had four bradycardia episodes; but even with the bradycardia scares, Lizzy said she was much happier after she got to hold her.

That evening Josh and Evan came to visit. The doctor told us that Grace had to be free of "brady" spells for at least forty-eight to seventy-two hours before she could be discharged, and we were not there yet. But we still got to care for her—bottles, rocking, baths, and changing diapers. Josh and Evan watched as I carefully fed Grace with our learned technique. Suddenly, Grace began to choke, her alarm sounded, and the screen flashed in red, *low heart rate*; and then her oxygen saturation levels dropped. The nurses, who always watched the monitors at the nurses' station, reacted quickly. Our nurse came running in. The charge nurse closely followed. They saw me trying to talk to Grace and rouse her, but it was not working. Grace began to turn red, then purple, and then gray. I looked for the emergency equipment. The nurse soon tore her from my arms and grabbed the ambu bag. I could see the oxygen level dropping lower and lower. Then the heart rate started to drop rapidly. All of the red blinking numbers were quickly going downward. The less I knew medically, the better off I would have been. They gave her oxygen and rubbed her sternum. It felt like hours. I was breathing hard and standing at the foot of the bed. It was a helpless feeling. We had to stand back and watch the life of our child slipping away, and we had to put our trust in strangers. In my head I repeated over and over, *Please God, no; please God, not yet. Please God help them!* Evan was saying, "Mommy, Mommy," and pulling at my leg. I could not believe he was there. I had to hold back my fear for him. I did not want him to know what was really going on, but I could not get myself to leave the room. I wanted him out of the room, but what was I supposed to do in that moment? I felt frozen, not knowing what to do. Every fraction of a second mattered. Finally, after a few minutes that felt like two hours, her levels began to climb into normal range. I was shaking and could not stop for a long time. I really thought we might lose her. As the nurses watched over Grace, I turned my eyes to Evan.

Evan began acting crazy, so I took him out into the playroom. He knew something was wrong. I let Josh finish feeding Grace; my nerves were shot. I could not even hold the bottle. Evan began to throw a horrible fit because he wanted to play the video games and other kids were playing them. The fit got worse. He began kicking, screaming, and hitting. I felt panicky. It was after 9 p.m. We were in a hallway full of sick kids. I did not want to be too harsh. I did not have the energy to be too harsh. But I could not leave him there on the floor screaming. Threats were not working. What was I supposed to do? I did not think it would look very good to sit on him and hold his mouth closed, although I sure thought about it. I felt like I was going to fall on the floor and scatter into pieces and someone would have to scoop me up.

Josh stepped in and took Evan to my parents. Then he came back. Josh and I slept in the little twin bed near Grace's crib. Every time Grace's alarm sounded, the nurses came running in. It was a busy night.

To make things worse, a big thunderstorm blew through that night. Two large windows reached to the ceiling right beside our bed. A huge clap of thunder startled me; then a lightning bolt blinded me. I fell out of the bed where we were crunched together. Luckily I was not hurt when I smacked the hard tile. We laughed about it. Even in the midst of fear and worry, God used his clap of thunder to give us a good laugh.

We needed that laugh because Grace had a rough night crying. She seemed to be in pain, and she had another spell. Music and rocking seemed to calm her some. I knew she was in pain, but there was nothing we could see and nothing the nurses could find. It was a helpless feeling. I was exhausted from the long night.

I talked with all of our family daily. Most of them called often or were there for a visit. My mother knew I was exhausted. She called to inform me early that morning that she and Jann had a plan to help with the baby. She was stern and told me I did not have a choice in the matter. I was way too tired to argue! I guess mothers are still mothers even when you are in your thirties. Mom still worked full-time and Jann had just retired. Mom offered to keep Evan and get him to day-care, while Jann would help at the hospital. The plan sounded good to me. I think I was ready for someone to just tell me what to do. Family members were the right people to do that.

Our family had not yet held Grace. We were trying to keep stimulation to a minimum and get Grace used to our smells and voices. We did not want to irritate Grace or cause any extra bradycardia episodes. We had read about how to help adopted children learn who their parents are. Adopted children usually do not hear their parents' voices often while they are in the womb. They are familiar with the sound of the birthmother. Naturally, when an infant is born, the mother's voice is familiar and calming. A lot of different voices and smells can be confusing and scary for a newborn. We had to put multiple holdings off for as long as possible. But it was time for help. Jann was ready for the challenge, so I taught her how to feed Grace.

On April 10—day twenty—life was moving along. Kristen, our NP, came in to discuss Grace's discharge. She said we could go home on a monitor or stay until we were comfortable. I wanted her to tell me what we should do. A week ago I would have been running out the door. But I was not keen on the idea of Grace having a major spell at home and having to perform CPR on my own child. Kristen went through all of the pros and cons. After some hesitation and contemplation we decided to go home. I was so ready to be with both of our children together, despite my fears concerning Grace's health. We learned how to use the home monitor that day and did in-room care. In-room care is when they allow the parents to do all of the care, but the nurses are still nearby if you need assistance. We even started using the home monitor instead of the complex hospital monitor. The monitor was the size of a purse with a shoulder strap. The gray wires went from the monitor to the two electrodes on Grace's chest. Jann stayed and helped since Josh was working. Josh wanted to be there the next day to take our baby girl home.

On Friday, April 11, 2008—day 21—we went home! At 5 pounds 13 ounces Grace looked like a peanut in her car seat. We carefully strapped her in with the help of the nurses. We placed her seat in a little red wagon with her monitor beside her. She had on her new outfit and cap. Our faces glowed as we rolled her through that hospital.

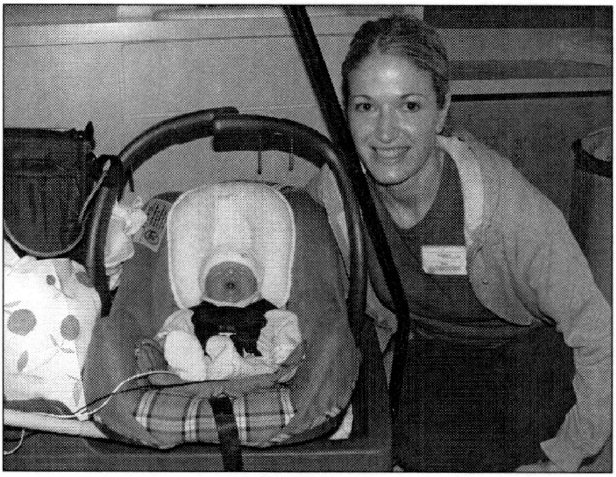

I sat beside her and watched her every move during the car ride home. When we arrived at our inviting home, there was a restful peace among us. It was our home where we were the ones in charge. We had no rules and could do what we saw fit. We moved some furniture and set up her bassinet and all of her medical supplies in our bedroom.

We had some scary moments with the monitor alarms. When Grace would stop breathing, her heart rate would drop. We just stimulated Grace by talking to her or touching her. Her breathing and heart rate would then go back to normal. We had a home health nurse scheduled to come to the house, and more medical supplies had been ordered.

Two days after arriving home, we went to see our pediatrician Dr. White. We had been seeing Dr. White since Evan was a baby, and I trusted her. She did a lengthy exam. She was pleased at how well Grace was doing. She had reviewed all of her records. We talked about what had happened with the CCAM and how that diagnosis was removed. We told her about the rest of the events during Grace's hospital stay. The talking paused, her eyebrows lifted, and she said, "Praise God, right?" I was so glad to hear that from her. Finally—a doctor willing to say the word *God*! She could not have said it better!

She talked to us about the risk of Grace getting an infection. She told us to avoid public outings until her two-month shots. She did not want us in crowds because of the risk of RSV and the damage that it could do. This was not bad news because we had assumed this already. I preferred to keep her in the house and in a "bubble" for a while anyway. We left that visit with smiles.

CHAPTER SIXTEEN

The Whole Picture

All of the blessings from Grace's story were beyond our greatest prayers. God "is able to do immeasurably more than all we ask or imagine, according to his power" (Ephesians 3:20). Our blessings throughout our journey are too many to describe in detail. My co-worker was the one who got all this started. Two people who were going through hard times were looking for the right parents to raise their baby. Their paths crossed with ours—two parents looking for a child to love. Our agency social worker went above and beyond her responsibilities to help us. Our lawyer knew exactly what to do. People were repeatedly placed in our paths at just the right times and places. There was the lady in the elevator, the respiratory therapist, the many medical professionals, and a NICU nurse for our own personal help. People from churches all over the country were praying for us and our baby Grace.

The nurses who cared for Grace touched her life, but she also touched theirs. I had a small pink paper notebook at Grace's bedside during her hospital stay for visitors and staff to write in. These were some of the comments written by the nurses who cared for Grace:

My little princess,

It has been a blessing to care for such a little miracle! You have come a long way in such a short time and I only know this is the start of great things to come. Stay strong and feisty. I will see you when I get back from my trip, just in time to see you out the door! Eat all your food and NO choking!

Dear Miss Grace,

I swear you are the cutest baby on "B" Pod. Everyone loves you, especially those of us lucky enough to get to care for you. Mom and Dad are so lucky to be getting such an amazing little girl. Keep growing big and strong! I'll be stopping by to check on you. Oh, and make sure your new nurses remember to match your bow to your adorable outfits. A baby girl's gotta have style, you know!

God Bless Baby Girl

Grace,

You are such a joy to take care of. People ask me all the time "How can you take care of sick babies?" and it's because of little miracles like you. You are a true blessing.

Grace,

It was a pleasure to take care of you these past few days. You are a sweet spirited little girl and you are very lucky to have such great parents and a big brother. You are a testimony of a modern day miracle.

Many people have been touched by Grace's story. I had placed Grace's adoption book at her bedside when we were still in the NICU. One of the nurses later told me that they passed it around to all of the NICU nurses during a night shift, and many of them read it. We didn't think much of it until we looked at it again and read the letter in which we had shared our thoughts on God and on Jesus as our Savior. When we had written that letter, we had no idea that so many strangers would read it. Maybe one seed was planted that night. Maybe one person thought about his or her faith.

We maintained our health despite lack of sleep, stress, and being in a hospital that closed down due to eighty cases of flu in one day. There are serious side effects that can occur from ventilators and many of the treatments that Grace received. She had none of them. Lizzy did not waiver in her decision, nor did the baby's birthfather. We had one of the best children's hospitals within driving distance from home.

To say the least, things get messy and dirty when you are rarely at your house for three weeks. My sister Stephanie, who hates cleaning her own house, cleaned my whole house so we would be able to rest when we got home from the hospital with Grace. We were so relieved we did not have to bring her home to a filthy pit. She even cleaned our microwave. Yuck! Cleaning my microwave was a brave service of love.

The nurse practitioner who took care of Grace after we left the hospital was caring, thorough, and extremely helpful with Grace's medical needs. We found out after a while that our fathers were good friends in the military—what a coincidence! We had financial help come in from places we never dreamed of. Because of our chance meeting with Danny, we have beautifully photographed memories. Danny's wife owns a photography business and came to our house soon after Grace arrived home to take pictures of Grace as a priceless gift to us. We also had Danny's great hugs at just the right time.

rainkite photography

Once we had her home, we wanted the best of everything for Grace. We were worried about her immunity and strength. I was not able to provide breast milk for optimal nutrition. It only takes a couple of bottles of breast milk per day to provide all of the benefits. You can buy it from a bank, but it is extremely expensive. It makes expensive formula look cheap. My friend Phoebe had a six-month-old baby she was weaning and donated her extra milk for Grace for an entire month. She even had her family deliver it so we did not have to freeze it. Now that was an extraordinary gift!

Evan was a wonderful big brother to his new baby sister. He was gentle, loving, and protective beyond my expectations. Josh was my constant source of earthly love, support, and strength. My amazing nieces and nephews—Andrew, Payton, Kenzy, and Ava—provided beautiful artwork for Grace's walls, brought life and fun to us, and said numerous innocent prayers. My parents, Steve and Mary, brought us food and cared for Evan. My sister and Brian also kept and cared for Evan frequently. Jann spent a lot of time helping us with laundry, chores, and caring for Grace. Josh's dad, Bob, continually visited and offered to help however he could. Josh's sister, Rachel, and Chris took Evan to Easter events with their kids. Our families stepped in and did far more than I could list or even remember!

Our friends and family helped us turn an empty brown room into a nursery fitting for a beautiful baby girl—lots of pink and flowers. They all provided clothes, diapers, and other items we needed for a new baby. They also fed us; they all knew eating was not high on our priority list. Several different friends also took Evan so he could have some special fun times while we were at the hospital.

Friends and family prayed for us, checked in often, and showered us with their love and support. These people were gifts from God, and we could not have made it through the difficult times without them all! It took every single piece of the puzzle, big and small, good and bad, to bring everything together to where we are today. God brought everything together for the greater good.

Because of Grace's journey, over fifty of our friends and family came together to help raise over $1000 for other babies like Grace. Maybe one baby was saved. Maybe more research was done. Over one hundred friends and family members came together to celebrate God's goodness in a special celebration service we held for Grace. Our pastor wrote Grace's story for the local newspaper. I know that Grace's story has reminded many of God's power. I am not sure we will ever fully understand all of the blessings and all of the purposes of Grace's miracle. The difficult times appeared like scribbles on paper. I can now look back and see where the scribbles began to turn into God's detailed masterpiece.

God can carry out His will in many ways. He can choose to do it through medications or medical treatments. He can choose to work through a doctor or scientist. Or He can choose to perform a miracle just to remind us that we are really not quite as advanced and smart as we think we are. God can also perform a miracle to remind us that He is in control.

Sometimes miracles never get shared with others. The social worker at Children's Health Hospital told us that she has seen unbelievable outcomes in their NICU. I don't know why more people don't tell their stories. Are they worried about what others will think? Sometimes things happen that we can't explain—isn't that okay? Doctors should never be afraid to say they cannot explain something. No human being can possibly know everything. Only God knows everything.

What is a miracle and what does it mean? My Bible dictionary defines a miracle as: *a divine act, unexplained by the laws of nature.* Many people use the word *miracle* inappropriately. Sometimes I feel like being able to get out of bed on a given day is a miracle, even though it is not a true miracle. But in Grace's story, God gave her a real miracle by definition. No doctor could clearly explain exactly what had happened. A few called it a miracle and another a medical mystery. No matter what word you use for it, modern science could not explain exactly what had happened.

No matter what diagnosis the doctors used to explain the x-rays or lung appearances, there were some simple facts. Grace was not removing amniotic fluid like she should have been, causing problems with pregnancy and labor. Grace had abnormal lung and heart appearances on all of her numerous sonograms and x-rays in the womb and after birth. Multiple specialists gave the same diagnosis. She could not breathe on her own when she was born. She required the most extensive life support available and was labeled as critical. Then, six days later, she was breathing completely on her own, and all of her other labs and her diagnosis tremendously improved that day. It fits the definition of miracle. On a Tuesday in March, 2008, God gave us His grace and a real modern day miracle. Our daughter Grace is living proof that miracles still happen.

"He rescues and he saves; he performs signs and wonders in the heavens and on the earth" (Daniel 6:27).

Afterward

We still had a lot of ups and downs with Grace's health. We knew Grace's life would not be absolutely perfect because she received a miracle—it was far from perfect! Grace's crying dragged us out of bed hourly, while we tripped over monitor wires and walked down a long flight of stairs to get bottles from the kitchen. Everywhere we carried Grace, the monitor went along. I had bruises from jumping up too quickly and running into walls when her alarm, which was louder than a fire alarm, would sound in the middle of the night. I had to stabilize my own heart rate and breathing after frantically working on hers.

I was weary and had to pray for strength to endure all of this without such grouchiness. Grace had difficulty sleeping and cried most of the time. Between her special care clinic, pediatricians, and ophthalmologist visits, we seemed to be at doctors' offices more than home. Twice on the way to an appointment, I had to dodge three lanes of traffic to jump into the car's back seat to stimulate my little blue Grace to breathe again. I often wondered how I made it through some of these circumstances without losing my sanity. I felt as if I had found strength that I did not know I had. "He gives strength to the weary and increases the power of the weak. Even youths grow tired and weary, and young men stumble and fall; but those who hope in the Lord will renew their strength" (Isaiah 40:29-30).

We were finally able to say a joyous good-bye to the breathing problems and the monitor at age five months, after Grace had a long period without any apnea or bradycardia spells. Grace was still on many medications. She was on preemie formula for twelve months. We had to keep her interested in eating so she would gain weight. She struggled with painful reflux and some GI issues for almost a year. Grace seemed to catch every cold and virus that was going around and required a lot of antibiotics. She had numerous ear infections and needed tubes placed in both ears. She was diagnosed with retinopathy, which typically happens in younger preemies. Retinopathy of prematurity (ROP) can potentially lead to blindness. We were fearful, but kept trying to remember our miracle. The retinopathy was gone two weeks after the diagnosis!

After her retinas matured, she was diagnosed with exotropia of both eyes. We had to put patches on her eyes to strengthen them. Keeping them on is no small feat for an eighteen-month-old baby! But even these issues were small compared to everything else she had been through and compared to what we were told she would have to go through.

As I finish this book, Grace is two-and-a-half years old. She has no health issues! She had successful surgery on her eyes this past summer for her exotropia. She is very social and seems to draw attention wherever she goes with her vibrant personality. She has the typical two-year-old behaviors (including full-fledged, kicking, flailing on the floor, screaming tantrums) and loves to hit her brother when she does not get her way. Despite her quick, toddler temper, Grace is always quick to say, "Sorry," and give hugs. Her lungs are healthy and open. Her lung capabilities are now so advanced that Josh can hear her voice across the superstore when Grace and I are at the opposite end. Her smile is bright and she is excited about life. Her eyes shine on her beautiful face. People often come to me and say, "There is just something special about Grace."

People whom I may never meet played a part in our story, but there is one woman I am glad I met. Her name is Irene. She lives in Michigan and has been a labor coach for years. She has helped to bring many babies into the world—from full term, healthy babies, to tiny, fragile, premature babies. In March of 2008 she wrote a poem about a fragile baby named

Grace whom she had never met, nor did she know this baby existed. I met Irene at a writers' conference in September of 2010, when my baby Grace was two years old. I told her my story; she showed me her poem. We both stared at each other. Tears filled our eyes and we were speechless.

Tuesday's Child

Beautiful Child
Planned Anticipated
Here you are

We name you Grace
Bright blue eyes draw me in
You capture my heart
You are exquisite
You are quiet
And do not squirm

Nagging worry grabs me
Too soon
Your breath is tentative
Not ready
You came too soon
Unfinished

But your will is evident
Hope was born on Tuesday
And we are optimistic
So much beauty
So much hope
This Tuesday's Child

Within minutes after I read this incredible poem, I met with Crystal, a talented speaker, author, and editor. She was told our story that same evening by a new friend. Crystal later accepted the major task of editing this book. She worked with enthusiasm and encouragement, and helped to turn this dream into reality. I met both of these women because another wonderful author, Penny Monetti, took the time to advise me and encourage me to attend this conference. I shared a dinner table with these three influential and talented women from three different states. I left that table with tears of thankfulness for these women that God placed in my life at just the right time. They all met different needs that I had. Once again I saw more evidence that God's fingerprints have been on Grace's life and story from the very beginning.

We keep in touch with Lizzy, John, and their families. We share pictures, e-mails, and have occasional visits. Grace's adoption has been a blessing to all of us, and Lizzy and John will always hold a very special place in our hearts.

We love to share the story of our modern day miracle with others. I have recorded our story so that the details will not be forgotten. I have also written our story so that others may be encouraged and find hope in God when they are going through desperate times. I hope that our story will give others the courage to pray for their miracle. "Let us then approach [God's] throne of grace with confidence, so that we may receive mercy and find grace to help us in our time of need" (Hebrews 4:16).

Howard Family November 2010
Grace 2 ½ and Evan 6
Photography by Mary Catherine Pringle

LaVergne, TN USA
07 March 2011
219048LV00001B/2/P

9 781612 155890